holy spirit 101

VICTORIA HARRIS

Arise Worship Ministry

———

Nihil obstat: Msgr. Robert M. Coerver, S.T.L., M.S.

Imprimatur: Most Reverend Bishop Kevin Joseph Farrell, Diocese of Dallas, February 15, 2016

———

Cover Design and layout by Corinne Alexandra

Holy Spirit 101 and other Arise Worship Ministry products are available at special quantity discounts for bulk purchases for sales promotions, premiums, fundraising, and educational needs. For details, write Mary Immaculate Publishing, 2800 Valwood Pkwy, Farmers Branch, TX, 75234 or visit www.ariseworshipministry.com

HOLY SPIRIT 101 by Victoria Harris
Published by Mary Immaculate Publishing/Arise Worship Ministry
2800 Valwood Pkwy
Farmers Branch, TX 75234
www.ariseworshipministry.com

contents

"*Whenever the Spirit intervenes, he leaves people astonished. He brings about events of amazing newness; he radically changes persons and history. This was the unforgettable experience of the Second Vatican Council during which, under the guidance of the same Spirit, the Church rediscovered the charismatic dimension of one of her constitutive elements: "It is not only through the sacraments and the ministrations of the Church that the Holy Spirit makes holy the people, leads them and enriches them with his virtues. Allotting his gifts according as he wills (cf. 1 Corinthians 12:11), he also distributes special graces among the faithful of every rank...He makes them fit and ready to undertake various tasks and offices for the renewal and building up of the Church" (Lumen Gentium, n.12).*"

– *Saint Pope John Paul II, Saturday May 30, 1998*

"*If we do not know the Spirit, then our knowledge of Jesus is only partial. Those who do not know the Holy Spirit have – dare I say – missed the point of Jesus' saving work.*"

– *Cardinal Donald Wuerl, Open to the Holy Spirit, p. 15*

"*...The gifts of the Spirit demand that those who have received them exercise them for the growth of the whole Church.*"

– *Christifideles Laici, 24*

FOREWORD

In the early winter months of 2015 I reached out to Victoria (Tori) Harris, at that time a frequent and recent visitor to Dallas and Mary Immaculate Parish, to ask her to consider relocating her home base of operations for her rising music ministry from New York City to Dallas, Texas. Tori had just left the comforts of her well known environment in Nashville, Tennessee, and had embarked on an intense period of discernment for God's will in her life and to choose a future place where she could call home.

My intention was to offer her a secure base of operations, a parish that would allow her the freedom to develop her already successful contemporary Catholic-Christian music ministry free from the anxieties of daily financial needs and demands. Plus, there's always plenty of work to be done in the parish and she could assist us with our evangelization efforts while continuing to develop her own music ministry.

I remember well the day she called me from New York several weeks after my initial offer of employment. It was my day off; I had just arrived at a ranch outside of Dallas where I would take in some country air and watch the cows graze. It was a cold and overcast day but our conversation brought a glimpse of springtime to come.

Tori proposed to me the idea of forming a parish based healing ministry grounded in utilizing the supernatural gifts of the Holy Spirit and in strict obedience to the teachings of the Catholic Church.

The ministry would train lay faithful on how to unleash or actualize the supernatural gifts of the Holy Spirit given to each of us at baptism. The gifts of healing, prophecy, tongues, discernment, deliverance, etc., are still at service to the Church but there didn't seem to be a theologically solid, single resource or process for promoting and using them.

While I am personally a beneficiary of the fruits of the Life in the Spirit Seminar, popular in the 1970's – 1980s, that program seems to have fallen by the wayside in most parishes, at least here in the Southwest. Perhaps the time was right for a new approach and a new resource.

Tori then asked me if my parish, Mary Immaculate, would be open to explore and possibly develop this new ministry. While not 100% sure what that would look like, I encouraged her to come to work at Mary Immaculate and we would explore the prospects of embarking on this new ministry. She accepted the offer.

Holy Spirit 101 (HS 101) is the fruit of that acceptance. This manuscript is the result of countless hours of compiling research, editing, praying, consulting, collaborating and networking with numerous people, clergy and laity, in order to achieve the aforementioned goal of providing a theologically sound resource for actualizing the supernatural gifts of the Holy Spirit.

This curriculum has proven to be successful in achieving its goals. As of this writing, merely a year and a half from that initial phone conversation, hundreds of people from Mary Immaculate, surrounding parishes and even other states have gone through the series and experienced the supernatural gifts of the Holy Spirit. People's lives have been touched and have been enhanced through attending the HS 101 sessions and retreats.

Furthermore, coupled with the monthly "Arise Night" where Adoration, Confession and Intercessory Prayer offers HS 101 participants and graduates the opportunity to use their newfound gifts, attendees at the Arise Nights are experiencing healing, forgiveness, consolation and receiving new insight as to the Lord's will in their lives.

It is a privilege to have played a seminal part in the genesis and development of this ministry. As a priest, a pastor, I am constantly pleased to witness the manner in which the Lord will orchestrate the bestowing of His blessings upon our Church.

HS 101 is another one of those orchestrations, another one of those blessings!

Rev. Michael D. Forge, Pastor
Mary Immaculate Parish
Dallas, Texas

course introduction

USING HOLY SPIRIT 101

0.1

THE HOLY SPIRIT ALIVE TODAY

Amen, amen, I say to you, whoever believes in me will do the works
that I do, and will do greater ones than these, because I am going to
the Father. And whatever you ask in my name, I will do, so that the
Father may be glorified in the Son. If you ask anything of me in my
name, I will do it.... And I will ask the Father, and he will give you
another Advocate to be with you always, the Spirit of truth, ... [who]
will be in you. (John 14:12–14, 16–17)

In 2010, *The Southern Medical Journal* published an article by a
group of scientists titled "Study of the Therapeutic Effects of Proximal Intercessory Prayer on Auditory and Visual Impairments in
Rural Mozambique."[1] *Proximal Intercessory Prayer* (PIP) is a term
coined by the authors of the article to refer to direct-contact prayer,

---

1 Candy Gunther Brown et al. "Study of the Therapeutic Effects of Proximal Intercessory
   Prayer." *Southern Medical Journal*, vol. 103, no. 9 (September 2010), pp. 864–869.

frequently involving touch, by one or more persons on behalf of another. It is more commonly known as "laying on of hands."

For this study, twenty-four Mozambican subjects with various hearing and vision impairments were evaluated. The scientists measured each subject's degree of disability. Then the subjects received, one-by-one, proximal intercessory prayer from a team led by Christian missionary Heidi Baker.

> ... They [the prayer team] placed their hands on the recipient's head and sometimes embraced the person in a hug, keeping their eyes open to observe results. In soft tones, they petitioned God to heal, invited the Holy Spirit's anointing, and commanded healing and the departure of any evil spirits in Jesus's name. Those who prayed then asked recipients whether they were healed. If recipients responded negatively or stated that the healing was partial, PIP was continued. If they answered in the affirmative, informal tests were conducted, such as asking recipients to repeat words or sounds (e.g., hand claps) intoned from behind or to count fingers from roughly 30 cm away. If recipients were unable or partially able to perform tasks, PIP was continued for as long as circumstances permitted.[2]

After the PIP sessions were completed, the scientists evaluated the subjects to determine the degree of healing (if any). Of the twenty-four total participants, one subject reported no improvement, three subjects were excluded from further analysis because of errors in their initial screenings, and two subjects were not able to receive

---

2   Brown et al, p. 865.

a follow-up analysis due to time constraints. The remaining eighteen participants all experienced restoration of audio or visual function.

> *Both auditory ... and visual ... improvements were statistically significant across the tested populations. Generally, the greater the hearing or vision impairment pre-PIP, the greater the post-PIP improvement.*[3]

In short, the study confirmed that prayer brings healing. The blind regained their sight, and the deaf began to hear. In a mysterious way, a spiritual reality manifested and altered the physical world. The prayer was so effective that the article, in its conclusion, recommended further study of PIP as a "useful adjunct to standard medical care ..., especially in contexts where access to conventional treatment is limited."[4]

What power moved in these Mozambique subjects to bring about such dramatic physical healing? What was so special about Heidi Baker and her prayer teams? Is the Catholic Church supportive or suspicious of these types of activities? And can this kind of miraculous episode of healing through prayer be repeated?

What you have in your hands is an introductory course that seeks to answer those questions. It presents not an exhaustive theology but rather a simple, practical tool for teaching about the gifts of the Holy Spirit in the context of Catholic parish life, particularly in the training of intercessory prayer teams. The themes covered are not original but rather reflections on the Holy Spirit birthed and stored within the treasury of Scripture and Tradition.

---

3   Brown et al, p. 867.
4   Brown et al, p. 868.

These teachings form a five-week program at Arise Worship Ministry in Farmers Branch, Texas. With the publication of this text, we hope to help other Catholics discover, develop, discern and share the gifts the Holy Spirit for the building up of the Church.

Come Holy Spirit, fill the hearts of your faithful
and kindle in them the fire of your love.
Send forth your Spirit, and they shall be created.
And you shall renew the face of the earth.

O, God, who by the light of the Holy Spirit,
did instruct the hearts of the faithful,
grant that by the same Holy Spirit, we may be truly wise
and ever enjoy his consolations. Through Christ Our Lord,
Amen.

0.2

THE FOUR PILLARS

There are four major components, or pillars, of *Holy Spirit 101*. The first is the **teaching** presented in these pages; the second is the ongoing development of the student's **prayer life**; the third is the individual's participation in the **community life** of the Church; and the fourth is the individual's gift of self in **stewardship** to the Church and the world at large.

Teaching

The five sessions in this text focus on different dimensions of study of the Holy Spirit:

1. Introduction to the Holy Spirit and the Charisms
2. Intercessory Prayer Teams
3. Deliverance Prayer
4. The Word Gifts: Tongues, Interpretation, and Prophecy
5. Healing Prayer

A typical teaching program is forty-five minutes of lecture followed by thirty to forty minutes of student practicum and fifteen minutes of group discussion. Given the density of the material, students are advised to be familiar with the particular session's readings prior to attending class. It is also recommended that groups meet regularly following the course to continue to study the material, incorporating it into prayer meetings and worship services.

At the end of each section is a "Reflect. Receive. Respond." box. We encourage students to *reflect* on the given questions, *receive* an answer in prayer, and then actively *respond* to what he or she may have received by making simple changes in lifestyle, thinking, or prayer life.

Each session closes with a series of suggested **practicums**. These activities provide opportunities to practice operating in the gifts of the Holy Spirit in the safe and supervised context of the class.

Personal Prayer

Central to the teaching is the incorporation of its concepts into the individual's prayer life. An optional workbook, *HS101 Prayer Workbook*, helps guide students in their prayer life throughout the five-week course. There are three components to the *HS101 Prayer Workbook*:

*A **Daily Prayer:*** Each week, the student will be asked to incorporate a specific daily prayer into his or her life.

Daily Reading: Daily spiritual readings complement the theology that is discussed in each session. These will help the individual grow in knowledge and understanding of the gifts of the Holy Spirit. Students are encouraged to read and meditate on these readings.

Weekly Challenge: A prayer challenge each week will introduce
students to various forms of Christian prayer.

While the prayer workbook portion of this course recommends specific
prayer activities, Arise Worship Ministry also honors the depth and
beauty of other prayers and devotions recognized by the Church. In no
way do the workbook prayer suggestions aim to replace these. We offer
the personal prayer workbook simply as a resource.

Lastly, central to the development of the individual's spiritual life
is the regular reception of the sacraments, most specifically the Holy
Eucharist and the sacrament of penance and reconciliation. It is the
assumption of this course that students are striving to remain in a state
of grace and actively participate in the sacramental life of the Church.

Community Life

Community life, particularly worshiping and praying as a community, is essential to the thriving Christian life.

> But God did not create man as a solitary, for from the beginning
> "male and female he created them" (Genesis 1:27). Their compan-
> ionship produces the primary form of interpersonal communion.
> For by his innermost nature man is a social being, and unless he re-
> lates himself to others he can neither live nor develop his potential.[5]

Thus it is encouraged that all members of this course make a personal
commitment to intentional involvement in a local parish community.

---

5   Vatican II, Pastoral Constitution on the Church in the Modern Word, *Gaudium et Spes*,
     no. 12, December 7, 1965, Vatican.va.

A further recommendation of this course is membership in a small group, Bible study, women's club, or men's group that is faithful to the teachings of the Church and meets regularly.

Stewardship

The Scriptures urge, "As each one has received a gift, use it to serve one another as good stewards of God's varied grace" (1 Peter 4:10). An integral teaching of the Catholic faith is the call to be a good Christian steward. The United States Conference of Catholic Bishops instructs:

> ... We are also obliged to be stewards of the Church—collaborators and cooperators in continuing the redemptive work of Jesus Christ, which is the Church's essential mission. This mission—proclaiming and teaching, serving and sanctifying—is our task. It is the personal responsibility of each one of us as stewards of the Church. All members of the Church have their own roles to play in carrying out its mission.[6]

We encourage all students to be good stewards of the gifts they have received from God. This stewardship can take many forms, such as:

- Leading or organizing a local or parish-based small group;
- Ministry to the sick or homebound;
- Serving at Mass as a reader, choir member, extraordinary Eucharistic minister, or other volunteer;
- Generous support—time, money, prayers, and personal service—to diocesan and parish programs.

---

6   United States Conference of Catholic Bishops, "To Be a Christian Steward: A Summary of the U.S. Bishops' Pastoral Letter on Stewardship," usccb.org.

At Arise Worship Ministry, we host a monthly night of Eucharistic Adoration. We encourage former students to participate as greeters, as organizers, and on intercessory prayer teams. This allows them an opportunity to exercise their developing charisms for the service of their local parish.

For more information on Arise Worship Ministry and other resources—such as *HS101 Prayer Journal*, teaching aids, and other developing programs—visit <u>ariseworshipministry.com</u>.

Veni Sancte Spiritus!

session 1

INTRODUCTION TO THE
HOLY SPIRIT & THE CHARISMS

1.1

A BRIEF HISTORY OF
THE HOLY SPIRIT

John answered them all saying, "I am baptizing you with water, but one mightier than I is coming. I am not worthy to loosen the thongs of his sandals. He will baptize you with the holy Spirit and fire." (Luke 3:16)

Biblical Origins

What the scientists were able to record in Mozambique was not something new or unique to the Christians there but rather something that has been around the Church from the beginning. This kind of miraculous healing through intercessory prayer began most notably on the Feast of Pentecost, when the Holy Spirit descended upon the apostles and those gathered in the Upper Room (see Acts 2:1; John 20:19).

"Let each one prepare oneself to receive the heavenly gift (of prophecy)... God grant that you may be worthy of the charism of prophecy." —St. Cyril of Jerusalem

The fruits of this outpouring of the Holy Spirit are well recorded in the Acts of the Apostles: Peter healed a lame man (see Acts 3:1–11) and raised the dead (9:36–41), the apostles performed many signs and wonders (5:12–16), and Paul cast out an evil spirit (16:16–18). These incredible and miraculous manifestations of the Holy Spirit helped the early Church to grow and spread.

Movements of the Holy Spirit continued to be recorded by contemporary writers of the early Church. St. John Chrysostom (c. 349–407) wrote, "Every church had many who prophesied," and Cyril of Jerusalem (c. 313–386) noted, "[I]t was very common for ordinary members of the faithful to act in the gifts of the Holy Spirit."

Around the time of St. Augustine (c. 354 – 430), however, it appears as if the regular use of the gifts had declined significantly if not disappeared entirely. "The sign [speaking in tongues] was given and then passed away. We no longer expect that those on whom the hand is laid … will speak in tongues."[7] St. John Chrysostom, who in his writings affirmed the common use of prophecy in the early Church, later complained that "the charisms are long gone."[8]

Historians offer varying explanations for the general decline in the activity of the Holy Spirit through the centuries. Some possible reasons

"The charismatic dimension needs the institutional safeguard from deception and error, so that it can bear long-term fruit for the body of Christ. On the other hand, the institutional dimension needs the charismatic for the full creativity of the Holy Spirit to be manifested in the Church in every age and for the Church to be constantly reminded of her dependence on the risen Lord and his Spirit." —Cardinal Joseph Ratzinger

---

7   St. Augustine, Homily 13 on the First Letter of John, in Philip Schaff, ed., *Early Church Fathers*, vol. 7, *Nicene and Post-Nicene Fathers, First Series*, trans. H. Browne (Buffalo, N.Y.: Christian Literature Publishing, 1888).
8   St. John Chrysostom, quoted in Fr. William Most, "The Gifts of the Holy Spirit," ewtn.com.

include the rise of the Montanist heresy[9] in the second century combined with abuses of the gifts of the Holy Spirit. These resulted in Church-sanctioned safeguards, which in some cases had the unintended consequence of stifling the spread of the gifts.

Others suggest the growing popularity of infant baptism as a reason for the decline in use of spiritual gifts. As the popularity of infant baptism grew, Christians would less often witness the dramatic change that the arrival of the Holy Spirit brought to an adult soul. Consequently, people's expectations of the power released at baptism began to decrease.

> "The institutional dimension and the charismatic dimension… are coessential to the divine constitution of the Church founded by Jesus, because they both help to make the mystery of Christ and his saving work present in the world." —Pope St. John Paul II, 1988

While the more dramatic signs and wonders became less common among the lay faithful, the activity of the Holy Spirit in the life of the Church remained. This *activity* is present in the infallibility of the pope when teaching *ex cathedra* and in the structural charisms of the Church (those of priests, bishops, and deacons). And charisms continued, most notably in the lives of the saints.

---

9   The Montanist heresy was a heresy popular in the second century. Its founder, Montanus, taught that individuals during prophetic utterances would become possessed by the Holy Spirit and would speak not as messengers of God but as persons possessed by God and unable to resist. The heresy caused great division for many reasons, most especially because of the incorrect teaching that a person's free will could be denied through the exercise of the charism and because it brought a disregard for obedience to Church authority. For example, in instances where the prophecy conflicted with Church teaching, Montanists would take the side of the prophecy, incorrectly believing the false prophet to have the higher authority. As Pope St. John Paul II wrote, "[N]o charism dispenses a person from reference and submission to the *Pastors of the Church*" (*Christifideles Laici*, no. 24).

St. Francis of Assisi (c. 1181–1226) healed the sick, St. Francis Xavier (c. 1506–1552) preached in tongues, St. Joseph of Cupertino (c.1603–1663) was known as the "flying saint" because of his gift of levitation, and Padre Pio (c.1887–1968) conversed with others' guardian angels. Many saints who operated in the charismatic dimension of the faith also initiated reform and revival within the Church. St. Benedict of Nursia (c. 480–550), who prophesied the death of King Totila, composed the Rule of St. Benedict, which was so influential that he is known as the founder of Western Monasticism. St. Teresa of Avila (c.1515–1582), whose many miracles included raising her nephew from the dead, is credited with leading the reform of the Carmelite order.

Vatican II and the Laity

So while the charisms of the Holy Spirit were still present in the Church, it seemed as if they became rare, appearing almost exclusively to saints and religious. Which begs the question: Could the charisms ever return as common among the laity, just as they were common in the early Church?

The answer came in 1962, when Pope St. John XXIII called for a Second Vatican Council. So rich are the writings of Vatican II on the nature of the gifts and charisms of the Holy Spirit that Pope St. John Paul II stated in a 1998 address that the Church had

"Renew Your wonders in this our day, as by a new Pentecost. Grant to Your Church that, being of one mind and steadfast in prayer with Mary, the Mother of Jesus, and following the lead of Blessed Peter, it may advance the reign of our Divine Savior, the reign of truth and justice, the reign of love and peace. Amen." —Pope St. John XXIII, Prayer for the Success of Vatican II

"rediscovered the charismatic dimension."[10] *Lumen Gentium*, one of the council's principal documents, offers a clear definition of the role and purpose of the charisms in the life of the faithful:

> *It is not only through the sacraments and the ministrations of the Church that the Holy Spirit makes holy the people, leads them and enriches them with his virtues. Allotting his gifts according as he wills (cf. 1 Cor. 12:11), he also distributes special graces among the faithful of every rank. By these gifts he makes them fit and ready to undertake various tasks and offices for the renewal and building up of the Church, as it is written, "the manifestation of the Spirit is given to everyone for profit" (1 Cor. 12:7). Whether these charisms be very remarkable or more simple and widely diffused, they are to be received with thanksgiving and consolation since they are fitting and useful for the needs of the Church....[11]*

Vatican II laid the groundwork for a renewal in the Holy Spirit. In 1967, just two years after the close of the council, a group of students and professors from Duquesne University went on retreat and began praying for a fresh outpouring of the Holy Spirit. Many students reported an "Upper Room" experience, similar to that of the apostles. Patti Gallagher Mansfield, one of the students present at the retreat, recalls, "Some were laughing, others crying. Some prayed in tongues,

---

10   Speech of the Holy Father Pope John Paul II, Meeting with Ecclesial Movements and New Communities, May 30, 1998, no. 4, vatican.va.

11   Vatican Council II, Pastoral Constitution on the Church, Lumen Gentium, no. 12, in Austin Flannery, *The Conciliar and Post Conciliar Documents*, vol. 1, *Vatican Council II* (New York: Costello, 1998), p. 363.

others (like me) felt a burning sensation coursing through their
hands.... We literally stumbled into charismatic gifts like prophecy,
discernment of spirits, and healing."[12]

Word spread, and the movement grew, soon becoming
known as the Catholic Charismatic Renewal. Over 150 million
Catholics worldwide have shared this extraordinary encounter with
the Holy Spirit. 2017 will mark its fiftieth year.

In the last half century, the Church has responded to the
need for more catechesis and resources to guide faithful Catholics
in a life of the Holy Spirit. A combination of these new encyclicals,
letters, and documents from the hierarchy help to paint a clear
picture for faithful Catholics as to what it means to participate
in a life of the Holy Spirit, as well as an orthodox response to the
outpouring of the Holy Spirit.

In 2004, Pope St. John Paul II, on the Eve of Pentecost, stated,
"Thanks to the Charismatic Movement, a multitude of Christians,
men and women, young people and adults, have rediscovered Pentecost as a living reality in their daily lives. I hope that the spirituality of Pentecost will spread in the church as a renewed incentive to
prayer, holiness, communion and proclamation."[13]

Are you ready to answer Pope St. John Paul II's request and
help the spirituality of Pentecost spread in the Church?

---

12   Patti Gallagher Mansfield, "The Duquesne Weekend," Catholic Charismatic Renewal of
     New Orleans, ccrno.org.

13   Pope St. John Paul II, Homily, Celebration of First Vespers of Pentecost., no. 3, May 29,
     2004, Vatican.va.

♦ Reflect. Receive. Respond.

- In what ways has the Holy Spirit been active in the Church throughout history?
- What are some reasons for the decline in the activity of the Holy Spirit amongst the laity?
- What has been your personal experience with the charisms of the Holy Spirit?

1.2

THE CHARISMS OF THE SPIRIT

Now in regard to spiritual gifts, brothers, I do not want you to be unaware. (1 Corinthians. 12:1)

Before Jesus Christ ascended into heaven, he promised, "But I tell you the truth, it is better for you that I go…. I will send him to you. And when he comes, he will convict the world in regard to sin and righteousness and condemnation" (John 16:7–8).

The "him" Jesus was referring to was the Third Person of the Holy Trinity, the Holy Spirit. However, it was never Jesus's intention for the Holy Spirit to do his great work independent of his Church. God desires and encourages our participation in salvation history. One way we can participate is by receiving the Holy Spirit through baptism and then allowing God to awaken the charisms of the Holy Spirit within us for the building up of the Church.

What Is a Charism?

The Church defines **charisms** as "graces of the Holy Spirit which directly or indirectly benefit the Church, ordered as they are to her building up, to the good of men, and to the needs of the world."[14] The charisms are often referred to as "gifts of the Holy Spirit."

> … *There are* … *special graces, also called* charisms *after the Greek term used by St. Paul and meaning "favor," "gratuitous gift," "benefit." Whatever their character—sometimes it is extraordinary, such as the gift of miracles or of tongues—charisms are oriented toward sanctifying grace and are intended for the common good of the Church. They are at the service of charity which builds up the Church.*[15]

There are two kinds of gifts of the Holy Spirit: personal and charismatic. The **personal** gifts are meant to sanctify the individual,[16] while the **charismatic** gifts are meant for the good of the community. For this study, we will focus on the charismatic gifts. A **charismatic gift** can be defined as "a manifestation of God's power and presence given freely for God's honor and glory and for the service of others."[17]

One of the beauties of this definition is the broadness and range of gifts that are included and counted among the charisms of the Holy Spirit. Popular charisms range from administration and hospitality to prophecy and healing.

---

14   *CCC* 799.

15   *CCC*, 2003. See Vatican II, *Lumen Gentium* 12; 1 Corinthians 12.

16   The personal, sanctifying gifts are wisdom, understanding, knowledge, counsel, fortitude, piety, and fear of the Lord (see Isaiah 11:2–3).

17   Msgr. Vincent Walsh, *A Key to Charismatic Renewal in the Catholic Church* (Merion, Pa.: Key of David, 1976), p. 43.

The Nine Gifts of the Holy Spirit

Of the various gifts of the Holy Spirit, St. Paul lists nine gifts as
regular ministries that should be present in every local church.
In *A Key to the Charismatic Renewal in the Catholic Church*, Msgr.
Vincent Walsh states:

> *He [St. Paul] realized that the Holy Spirit regularly manifested
> Himself in these nine ways. St. Paul wanted the Early Christians to
> be familiar with these regular manifestations, to learn about them,
> to expect them and to yield to them all. In fact, he expected all
> nine gifts to be present in each Christian community. The absence
> of these gifts would signify some weakness in the Church's power.*[18]

Msgr. Walsh organizes the nine gifts in the following way:[19]

The Word Gifts (The Power to Say)

The Gift of Tongues: Whereby the person gives God's message,
in a language unknown to him, for the community present.

The Gift of Interpretation: Whereby a person, after the use
of the gift of tongues, gives the general meaning of what the
person has said, or a response to what has been said. Interpretation can also be used privately in conjunction with the gift
of prayer tongues.

---

18   *Walsh*, p. 44.
19   *Walsh*, pp. 43–44.

The Gift of Prophecy: Whereby the person gives God's message in the vernacular for the community or for an individual.

The Sign Gifts (The Power to Do)

The Gift of Faith: Which enables the person at a given moment to believe, and to call upon God's power with a certainty that excludes all doubt.

The Gift of Healing: Which enables the person to be God's instrument in bringing about the well-being of another, on one or more levels, spiritual, psychological or physical.

The Gift of Miracles: Which enables a person to be God's instrument in either an instant healing or some other powerful manifestation of God's power.

The Intellectual Gifts (The Power to Know)

The Word of Wisdom: Whereby a person is granted an insight into God's plan in a given situation and is enabled to put this into words of advice or of direction.

The Word of Knowledge: Whereby a person is granted an insight into a divine mystery or facet of man's relation to God and is enabled to put this into a word that helps others to grasp the mystery.

The Gift of Discernment: Whereby a person is enabled to know the source of an inspiration or action, whether it came from the Holy Spirit, [from] his own human spirit or from [an] evil spirit.

Defining Elements of Charismatic Gifts

These nine gifts share common defining elements. It is helpful to refer to these elements when discerning if a gift is, in fact, charismatic.

1. The gift is given freely to the individual.
2. While an individual may exercise a charism with frequency, the individual never personally possesses the power of the gift.
3. The gift is always exercised with the full consent of the will of the individual.
4. The gift brings about God's honor and glory.
5. The gift is for the service of others.
6. The gift is supernatural.

To expound further on these defining elements:

The gift is given freely to the individual. An individual cannot purchase, inherit, or earn the gifts. All gifts are given freely, by the Holy Spirit, to the individual. "From the beginning ... baptism in the Spirit has been experienced as a sovereign gift of God, not dependent on any human merit or activity."[20]

---

20   Doctrinal Commission of International Catholic Charismatic Renewal Services (IC-CRS), *Baptism in the Holy Spirit* (Locust Grove, Va.: NSC Chariscenter: 2012), p. 14.

While an individual may exercise a charism with frequency, the individual never personally possesses the power of the charism.
An individual cannot possess a charismatic gift, so in a sense, *gifts* is not the best word to express God's action. The charisms are "'ways in which God regularly manifests Himself through an individual." Therefore it is sometimes better to say that "a person 'yields' to a gift rather than 'has' a gift."[21]

The gift is always exercised with the full consent of the will of the individual. Even in the most intense and extraordinary manifestations of a charism, the individual retains his or her free will.

The gift brings about God's honor and glory. The gifts of the Holy Spirit do not bring honor to ourselves but bring honor to God. An indicator of a false gift or abuse of a genuine gift is an individual's use to draw attention to self and distract attention from God.

The gift is for the service of others. God grants the charisms to help build his Church. "These charisms are understood as gifts not primarily for the recipient but for the building up of the Church and the work of evangelization."[22]

The gift is supernatural. A gift of the Holy Spirit stands apart from our natural gifts and talents. "[The gifts of the Holy Spirit are] not merely natural endowments or acquired skills, but supernatural gifts that either enable what is humanly impossible (such as healing or miracles) or enhance a natural gift to a level of supernatural efficacy."[23]

---

21   Walsh, p. 49.

22   ICCRS, p. 20.

23   ICCRS, p. 45.

◆ Reflect. Receive. Respond.

- What charisms are most attractive to you?
- Have you ever encountered someone exercising one of the nine charisms? What was that experience like?

1.3

THE OUTPOURING OF
THE HOLY SPIRIT

"Today, I would like to cry out to all of you gathered here in St. Peter's Square and to all Christians: Open yourselves docilely to the gifts of the Spirit! Accept gratefully and obediently the charisms which the Spirit never ceases to bestow on us!"

—Pope St. John Paul II[24]

Outpouring Defined

Stories such as those of the Christians in Mozambique often awaken within members of the faithful a desire to share in a similar experience. The experience of an indwelling of the Holy Spirit is not only free and available to every member of the Christian community but a promise

---

24 Pope St. John Paul II, Speech for the World Congress of Ecclesial Movements and New Communities, no. 5, June 3, 1998, Vatican.va.

of God the Father. "[W]ait for 'the promise of the Father about which you have heard me speak'; for John baptized with water, but in a few days you will be baptized with the holy Spirit" (Acts 1:4–5).

The Doctrinal Commission of International Catholic Charismatic Renewal Services (ICCRS) states: "By calling the Holy Spirit the 'promise of the Father,' Jesus indicated that the Spirit's coming will be the definitive fulfillment of God's promises (cf. Ezek 36:27; Joel 2:28–29), the culmination of his messianic mission."[25] St. Paul encourages the faithful to recognize their inclusion in this

> **What is the Outpouring of the Holy Spirit?**
> "[A]n internal religious experience (or prayer experience) whereby the individual experiences the risen Christ in a personal way. This experience results from a certain 'release' of the powers of the Holy Spirit, usually already present within the individual by Baptism and Confirmation." —Msgr. Vincent Walsh

promise: "Pursue love, but strive eagerly for the spiritual gifts" (1 Corinthians 14:1).

So if the gifts are for everyone, and promised by the Father, how does one receive them? In truth, the answer is very simple: An individual receives the indwelling of the Holy Spirit by virtue of their baptism and confirmation.[26] **If a Christian has received these sacraments, the Holy Spirit is already present.**

Though the sacraments of baptism and confirmation bestow upon an individual the gift of the indwelling of the Holy Spirit, "many powers associated with this indwelling are bound up, untapped so to speak. A 'release of the power of the Spirit' means that the full effects

---

25   ICCRS, p. 34.

26   Note: It is possible for an individual to receive the outpouring of the Holy Spirit prior to baptism; however, it should lead the person to be baptized sacramentally. For example, the Gentile Cornelius and his family experienced the full outpouring of the Spirit, and Peter responded by immediately baptizing them into the Christian community (see Acts 10:44–48).

of the sacraments are actually realized, as the Spirit leads the Christian into a new life of prayer, of outlook and of behavior."[27]

There are many names and colloquial terms for this outpouring of the Holy Spirit, including baptism of the Spirit, effusion of the Spirit, awakening of the Spirit, and others. For the purposes of this course, we will refer to the experience as the "outpouring of the Holy Spirit."

> "I expect from you that you share with all, in the Church, the grace of Baptism in the Holy Spirit." —Pope Francis to the 37th Convocation of Renewal, June 1, 2014

Receiving the Outpouring of the Holy Spirit

> *Therefore, you blessed ones, for whom the grace of God is waiting, when you come up from the most sacred bath of the new birth, when you spread out your hands for the first time in your mother's house (the church) with your brethren, ask your Father, ask your Lord, for the special gift of his inheritance, the distribution of charisms, which form an additional, underlying feature (of baptism). "Ask," he says, "and you shall receive." In fact, you have sought and it has been added to you.*
>
> —Tertullian, On Baptism[28]

As the Holy Spirit is already present in the baptized and confirmed person, He may be "awakened" at any time and under any circumstance. The outpouring happens either privately or publicly.

---

27   Walsh, p. 24.

28   *"Igitur benedicti quos gratia dei expectat, cum de illo sanctissimo lavacro novi natalis ascenditis et primas manus apud matrem cum fratribus aperitis, petite de patre, petite de domino, peculia gratiae distributiones charismatum subiacere; petite et acceipietis inquit; quaesistis enim et invenistis, pulsastis et apertum est nobis." On Baptism* 20; SC 35:96.

In a **private outpouring**, the Christian, during personal prayer, experiences an awakening of the Spirit. This occurs either spontaneously or after intentionally petitioning the Holy Spirit to awaken the charisms. For example, during a private holy hour of adoration, Suzie feels an unexplainable urge to speak, and as she does, she senses an overwhelming power of the Holy Spirit and realizes that she's praying in tongues.

In a **public outpouring**, the individual is surrounded by members of a community who specifically and intentionally pray for the outpouring of the Spirit in the person's life. In *A Key to the Charismatic Renewal* in the Catholic Church, Msgr. Walsh describes a typical public outpouring:

> *Members of the community usually impose hands upon him as a fraternal gesture (although this is not absolutely necessary). The leader says a prayer of deliverance, followed by a petition that... the person realize all the effects, devotional and charismatic.*[29]

Quite simply, to receive the outpouring of the Holy Spirit, the Christian, whether alone or in community, must simply ask God for it and believe that God has answered his petition. "[W]e should believe in faith that, if the person was properly disposed, he did receive the Baptism [outpouring] of the Holy Spirit and need not be prayed for again."[30]

---

29   Walsh, p. 29.
30   Walsh, p. 30.

Waiting for the Promise of the Father

There are signs that typically accompany an outpouring of the Holy Spirit:

- the emergence of the gift of tongues or other charisms
- a deeper hunger and thirst for prayer
- a desire to read Scripture
- power over sin and evil habits
- detachment from material goods
- growth in union with God

An individual might not experience all of these signs. Indeed, he or she might not experience any of them. This can lead to disappointment and even doubt regarding the efficacy of his or her prayer. In such a situation, it is good to refer to Jesus's command to the apostles in Acts 1:4, to wait for the promise of the Father.

In this call to "wait," Jesus shows that the coming of the Spirit is not under human control. God will pour out his Spirit when and how he wills. "Acts depicts the one hundred and twenty disciples gathered in the upper room as disposing themselves to receive the Spirit through their perseverance in prayer."[31] The Christian eager to enter into the charisms of the Holy Spirit can follow the example of those in the Upper Room by remaining in a state of grace, making a good confession, and continuing to persevere in prayer.

In the laying on of hands now, that persons may receive the Holy Ghost, do we look that they should speak with tongues? Or when we laid the hand on these infants, did each one of you look to see

---

31   Walsh, p. 34.

whether they would speak with tongues, and, when he saw that they did not speak with tongues, was any of you so wrong-minded as to say, These have not received the Holy Ghost; for, had they received, they would speak with tongues as was the case in those times? If then the witness of the presence of the Holy Ghost be not now given through these miracles, by what is it given, by what does one get to know that he has received the Holy Ghost? Let him question his own heart. If he love his brother the Spirit of God dwells in him.

—*St. Augustine of Hippo*[32]

◊ Reflect. Receive. Respond.

- Have you prayed for an outpouring of the Holy Spirit in your life? Why or Why not?
- How would you encourage a friend or family member to pray for an outpouring of the Holy Spirit?

---

32   St. Augustine of Hippo, Homily on the First Letter of John, in Schaff, p. 498

1.4

GROWING IN THE SPIRIT

Now you are Christ's body, and individually parts of it. Some people God has designated in the church to be, first, apostles; second, prophets; third, teachers; then, mighty deeds; then gifts of healing, assistance, and administration, and varieties of tongues. (1 Corinthians 12:27–28)

Just as there are many ways of life and paths to holiness for Catholics (marriage, priesthood, religious life, and so on), there are also many ways for an individual to grow in the gifts of the Holy Spirit. Below is a suggestion for individual growth.

Cycle of Spiritual Growth

PREPARE

PRACTICE

IDENTIFY

LEARNING

Prepare

Consider the farmer: Before a farmer can go out and plant crops, he must prepare the fields so that the seeds have the best chance to grow. So it is with the charisms of the Holy Spirit in the lives of the faithful. Seeds planted in good soil will take root and bear fruit a hundredfold (see Mark 4:18). To ensure continued growth in a charism, the individual must constantly prepare the soil of his or her soul.

To prepare one's soul, consider the following suggestions:

1. Strive to remain free from sin and in a state of grace. Avoid temptation, go to confession regularly, renounce occult activities.
2. Participate in the sacramental life of the Church. Receive the Eucharist often.
3. Cultivate a daily prayer life.
4. Pray often with others, especially those who are also seeking to grow in the gifts of the Holy Spirit.
5. Ask God in prayer for the gifts of the Holy Spirit.
6. Be obedient to the promptings of the Holy Spirit.

Identify

When desiring to grow in the gifts of the Holy Spirit, it is helpful for the individual to first identify what gift he/she desires to grow in. For how can we grow in a gift if we don't know what that gift is?

Sometimes the movement of the Holy Spirit is so dramatic that it is obvious that a particular charism is present. Other times, the movement of the Spirit is subtle, passing unnoticed. Or because of lack of knowledge, an individual is unaware that he or she is acting in a charism.

In cases where charisms are difficult to discern, it may be
helpful to consult a charism list or quiz (for example, Sherry Weddell's "Spiritual Gifts Inventory") and to seek the counsel of a trusted
spiritual director.[33]

Learn

Choose the charism you want to test and try to approach it ob-
jectively. Learn as much as you can about it. Specifically, what the
Church teaches about the charism and how to exercise it within
Church teaching and tradition.

Practice

There is no definitive way to begin using a charism, and the Church
does not offer a foolproof how-to guide. A lot of an individual's experience with the Holy Spirit will grow through a mix of education
and trial and error. Here are some tips:

1. *Experiment thoroughly with the gift by using it.* For example,
   if the gift is healing, offer to pray for sick persons; if the gift is
   administration, offer to help coordinate a parish event.
2. *Seek out others who have this gift.* Pray with them, learn from
   them, and share your experience with them. "As iron sharpens
   iron, so man sharpens his fellow man." (Proverbs 27:17)
3. *Examine your inner experience while exercising the gift.* Pay
   particular attention to the fruits of the Spirit: peace, joy, charity,

---

33 See Sherry Weddell, *The Catholic Spiritual Gifts Inventory: Helping Catholics Succeed at a
    Primary Discipline of the Christian Life* (Colorado Springs: Siena, 1998).

patience, kindness, goodness, generosity, gentleness, self-control, modesty, and chastity.

4. ***Evaluate your actual effectiveness.*** What is happening when you pray? Are you effectively demonstrating the charism?

5. ***Weigh the responses of others.*** Seek the counsel of your spiritual director and religious leaders. Ask for feedback from those with whom you pray.

6. ***Remain in obedience.*** The Holy Spirit instituted the offices of the Church and will not operate in contradiction to her. "And if a house is divided against itself, that house will not be able to stand" (Mark 3:25). The gifts of the Holy Spirit should always be practiced in a manner recognized by and in line with the teachings of the Church.

Above all, be patient and persevere. Just as it takes years for a sapling to become a great tree, it can take many years for the charisms of the Holy Spirit to fully manifest in an individual. As Hilary of Poitiers writes, "We begin to have insight into the mysteries of faith, we are able to prophesy and to speak with wisdom. We become steadfast in hope and receive the gifts of healing…. These gifts enter us as a gentle rain. Little by little they bear abundant fruit."[34]

---

34   Hilary of Poitiers, *Tract on Psalms* 64:15, as quoted in McDonnell and Montague, p. 17.

◆ Reflect. Receive. Respond.

- In what ways are you preparing your soul to receive the gifts of the Holy Spirit?

- How important is obedience to the Church for the growth of the gifts of the Spirit? In what areas of your life are you living in obedience to the Church? In what areas are you disobedient?

practicum

FOR SESSION 1

exercise 1

PRAYING FOR THE OUTPOURING
OF THE HOLY SPIRIT

Directions

It is best to have a trained team of intercessors available to pray
with students; however, simple prayers from students will also
suffice. If the individual does not want to approach a prayer team,
he or she can complete the exercise individually.

Step 1

Allow students to spend five minutes preparing themselves individually
for the prayer session. Some questions may help students prepare:

- Do I believe in the Holy Spirit?
- Do I believe that I received the Holy Spirit at my baptism and
  was sealed with the Holy Spirit at my confirmation?
- Do I believe that the Holy Spirit can move through the people
  of his Church?
- To what charisms or gifts of the Holy Spirit am I most attracted?

Step 2

Allow students, one by one, to come to the front of the room and
receive prayer. Have the prayer team petition God, in a calm and
orderly way, for a greater outpouring of the Holy Spirit in the
student's life. Have the student verbally petition God as well.

Step 3

When a student completes his or her time in a prayer session, that individual may pray silently, journal, or join a prayer team in praying for another student.

Step 4

Come together as a group for sharing and discussion.

Notes:

_____

_____

_____

_____

_____

_____

_____

session 2

INTERCESSORY PRAYER TEAMS

2.1

THE POWER OF PRAYER

Therefore I tell you, all that you ask for in prayer, believe that you will receive it and it shall be yours. (Mark 11:24)

"[Saint] Scholastica, the sister of Saint Benedict, had been consecrated to God from her earliest years. She was accustomed to visiting her brother once a year. He would come down to meet her at a place on the monastery property, not far outside the gate.

One day she came as usual and her saintly brother went with some of his disciples; they spent the whole day praising God and talking of sacred things. As night fell they had supper together. Their spiritual conversation went on and the hour grew late. The holy nun said to her brother: "Please do not leave me tonight; let us go on until morning talking about the delights of the spiritual life." "Sister," he replied, "what are you saying? I simply cannot stay outside my cell."

When she heard her brother refuse her request, the holy woman joined her hands on the table, laid her head on them and began to pray. As she raised her head from the table, there were such brilliant flashes of lightning, such great peals of thunder and such a heavy downpour of rain that neither Benedict nor his brethren could stir across the threshold of the place where they had been seated. Sadly he began to complain: "May God forgive you, sister. What have you done?" "Well," she answered, "I asked you and you would not listen; so I asked my God and he did listen. So now go off, if you can, leave me and return to your monastery." Reluctant as he was to stay of his own will, he remained against his will. So it came about that they stayed awake the whole night, engrossed in their conversation about the spiritual life.

It is not surprising that she was more effective than he, since as John says, God is love. It was absolutely right that she could do more, as she loved more.

Three days later, Benedict was in his cell. Looking up to the sky, he saw his sister's soul leave her body in the form of a dove, and fly up to the secret places of heaven. Rejoicing in her great glory, he thanked almighty God with hymns and words of praise. He then sent his brethren to bring her body to the monastery and lay it in the tomb he had prepared for himself.

Their minds had always been united in God; their bodies were to share a common grave."[35]

---

35   Excerpt from St. Gregory the Great, *Dialogues*, bk. 2, chap. 33, "Of a Miracle Wrought by His Sister Scholastica."

◊ Reflect. Receive. Respond.

- When was the last time you prayed for God to intervene in a miraculous way?
- What do you think made St. Scholastica's prayer so effective?

2.2

PRAYER DEFINED

*Have no anxiety at all, but in everything, by prayer and petition, with
thanksgiving, make your requests known to God. Then the peace
of God that surpasses all understanding will guard your hearts and
minds in Christ Jesus. (Philippians 4:6-7)*

According to St. John Damascene, **prayer** is "the raising of one's
mind and heart to God or the requesting of good things from God."[36]
There are many forms of prayer (for example, meditation, vocal
prayer, and contemplation), and there are many reasons to pray
(thanksgiving, adoration, contrition, and supplication).
Certain prayers are reserved for those
holding a certain office (such as the
Eucharistic Prayer, reserved for
priests), other prayers are available to

*"I pray for them. I do not pray for the
world but for the ones you have given
me, because they are yours." —John 17:9*

---

36   St. John Damascene, *De fide orthodoxa* 3, 24: PG 94, 1089C, as quoted in CCC 2559.

any member of the general public (for example, the rosary and the Divine Office), and some prayers are reserved to a Church season or particular celebration (baptismal blessings and home blessings, for example).

"Contemplative prayer in my opinion is nothing else than a close sharing between friends; it means taking time frequently to be alone with him who we know loves us." —St. Theresa of Avila, quoted in CCC 2709

In short, prayer is diverse, fluid, and living. Yet, despite the vast differences in the types of prayer, there is one Spirit who unites them all:

The Holy Spirit, whose anointing permeates our whole being, is the interior Master of Christian prayer. He is the artisan of the living tradition of prayer. To be sure, there are as many paths of prayer as there are persons who pray, but it is the same Spirit acting in all and with all. It is in the communion of the Holy Spirit that Christian prayer is prayer in the Church.[37]

"For me, prayer is a surge of the heart; it is a simple look turned toward heaven, it is a cry of recognition and of love, embracing both trial and joy." —St. Thérèse of Lisieux, quoted in CCC 2558

In this session, the reader is going to learn about **intercessory prayer** and how we are called as Christians to participate with the Holy Spirit in the good work of praying for others.

Intercessory Prayer

The Gospel of Mark gives us the famous story of the paralytic:
Unable to get near Jesus because of the crowd, they opened up the roof above him. After they had broken through, they let down the

37   CCC 2672.

mat on which the paralytic was lying. When Jesus saw their faith,
he said to the paralytic, "Child, your sins are forgiven." (Mark 2:4–5)

What makes this story so relevant to intercessory prayer is the last line, "When Jesus saw *their* faith, he said to the paralytic, 'Child, your sins are forgiven.'" The

> "In this intimate union [prayer], God and the soul are fused together like two bits of wax that no one can ever pull apart." —St. John Vianney, Catechetical Instructions

healing of the paralytic did not come by the paralytic's accord. The paralytic did not bring himself to Jesus. The paralytic needed help and friends; he needed community. It was *their* faith, the faith of the friends, that led Jesus to say, "Child, your sins are forgiven."

Sometimes in our lives we too become paralyzed to different wounds or sins. Like the paralytic in the Gospel story, we are unable to come to Jesus on our own. In these cases, intercessory prayer and intercessory prayer teams can be like the friends who brought the paralytic to Jesus.

What is intercessory prayer? The *Catechism of the Catholic Church* defines intercession as "a prayer of petition which leads us to pray as Jesus did."

> *He is the one intercessor with the Father on behalf of all men, especially sinners [see Romans 8:34; 1 John 2:1; 1 Timothy 2:5–8].... The Holy Spirit "himself intercedes for us ... and intercedes for the saints according to the will of God" [Romans 8:26–27].[38]*

---

38   CCC 2634.

Intercession is petitioning God in the place of another person.

> ... *Intercession implies that a person is unable or unwilling to*
> *petition God on his own behalf (Rm 8:26) and that the Lord*
> *sometimes permits us to substitute for others in prayer. Because*
> *God has given us authority (Gn 1:28) that He will not usurp,*
> *and because He will not usually impose His blessings on us,*
> *intercession makes a great difference. We don't receive because*
> *we don't ask (James 4:3). Intercession often is the difference*
> *between life and death, war and peace, healing or sickness,*
> *success or failure.*[39]

"Do not weep, for I shall be more useful to you after my death and I shall help you then more effectively than during my life." —St. Dominic, quoted in CCC 956

Praying on behalf of others was a practice of the first Christian communities. They interceded "'for all men, for kings and all who are in high positions' [1 Timothy 2:1–2], for persecutors, for the salvation of those who reject the Gospel."[40] Our Church leaders still recognize the importance of intercessory prayer. On the one-year anniversary of his election, Pope Francis stood in front of a great crowd, asking "that you would pray to the Lord to bless me—the prayer of the people for their Bishop."[41]

It makes great sense that this practice is prevalent both in the early Church and today, because it is a foretaste of heaven. The

---

39   Presentation Ministries, *Ten Commandments of Intercession* brochure (Cincinnati: Presentation Ministries, 2015) presentationministries.com.

40   CCC 2636.

41   Pope Francis, as quoted in "Pope Francis Asks on One Year Anniversary: 'Please Pray for Me,'" *Huffington Post*, March 13, 2014, huffingtonpost.com.

Church teaches, "Being more closely united to Christ, those who dwell in heaven fix the whole Church more firmly in holiness.... [T]hey do not cease to intercede with the Father for us."[42] Intercessory prayer could thus be called one of the ultimate ministries in the Church.

> ... *Jesus forever lives to make intercession for us (Heb 7:25). He lived a simple life in Nazareth for thirty years and had a public ministry for three years. And now He has been interceding for us for almost two thousand years. That may tell us something of the inestimable importance of intercession.*[43]

Intercessory prayer can take place in two ways: remotely or face-to-face.

- **Remote prayer** is praying for someone who is not presently with us.
- **Face-to-face prayer** is intercessory prayer in the presence of the person receiving prayer.

Our Collective Responsibility

In the parable of the talents (see Matthew 25:14–30), we learn that when God gives us a gift, we are to invest and use that gift. When we are faithful with what little God gives us, his response is to give us more. "For to everyone who has, more will be given and he will grow rich; but from the one who has not, even what he has will be taken away" (Matthew 25:29).

---

42 *CCC* 956, quoting *Lumen Gentium*, 49.
43 Presentation Ministries.

Charisms are gifts from the Holy Spirit. When we practice them through face-to-face intercessory prayer, we make a public witness to Christ's saving work and participate in the missionary life of the Church. We are called to embrace this work, not with a spirit of timidity but rather with great faith and missionary zeal.

Just as Jesus prays to the Father and gives thanks before receiving his gifts, so he teaches us filial boldness: "Whatever you ask in prayer, believe that you receive it, and you will" [Mark 11:24]. Such is the power of prayer and of faith that does not doubt: "All things are possible to him who believes" [Mark 9:23; see Matthew 21:22]. Jesus is as saddened by the "lack of faith" of his own neighbors and the "little faith" of his own disciples as he is struck with admiration at the great faith of the Roman centurion and the Canaanite woman [see Mark 6:6; Matthew 8:26; 8:10; 15:28]. [44]

◖ Reflect. Receive. Respond.

- How is intercession different from other types of prayer?
- When have you used intercessory prayer in your personal ministries?
- How can you pray with more "filial boldness"?

---

44   *CCC* 2610.

2.3

STEPS OF FACE-TO-FACE INTERCESSORY PRAYER

First of all, then, I ask that supplications, prayers, petitions, and thanksgivings be offered for everyone. (1 Timothy 2:1)

The gifts of the Holy Spirit are given for the building up of the Church and thus often manifest themselves during face-to-face intercessory prayer. Because this kind of prayer involves other people, it is important to be properly prepared, pastoral, and constantly considerate of the hearts and souls of individuals receiving prayer.

Through the years, the Church has instituted many safeguards, recommendations, rules, and guidelines for intercessory prayer. Yet because prayer is so individual (depending upon the person, culture, time, and season), a repeatable formula, that covers all areas and concerns of intercessory prayer, cannot exist. While taking this into consideration, the following recommendations are the norm for Arise prayer ministry teams.

At all times, remember that the *goal* of intercessory prayer is to bring the individual into union with God. The highest expression of this union is the reception of the sacraments of the Church, particularly the Eucharist. Greater union is also forged when an individual experiences consolation, deliverance from evil, a sense of the love and power of God, and repentance.

The Three Phases

Intercessory prayer can be divided into three unique phases:
1. Preparation Phase
2. Prayer Phase
3. Post-Care Phase

Preparation Phase

Face-to-face intercessory prayer begins long before one meets and begins to pray for another. Our lives should be in continual preparation for intercessory prayer.

Section 1.4 offered general guidelines of personal preparation for life in the Spirit. The following suggestions expand on that list:

1. ***Be in a state of grace:*** If you are in a state of mortal sin, become right with the Church. Make regular confessions, and receive the sacraments with frequently.

2. ***Have a prayer life:*** Personal daily prayer prepares you for moments of intercessory prayer. Have an established, regular, daily prayer life. Fasting is also particularly powerful.

Choose something you can fast from daily and offer this up for your face-to-face intercessory prayer ministry.[45]

3. *Belong to a friend group or ministry that prays together regularly:* These groups are especially efficacious because they are safe places to discover, discern, and develop new spiritual gifts, which can be introduced into public prayer ministry. They are also places where others hold us accountable.

4. *Examine your present state and discern if God is calling you into prayer ministry:* Are you currently suffering from trauma, addiction, or a compulsion? If so, this is a time for the Church to minister to you during your time of need. This is not an appropriate time to enter into public prayer ministry.

5. *Consider hygiene and personal appearance:* If you are going to be close to someone, have good breath, avoid perfumes and colognes, and present a clean appearance.

6. *Ask others to intercede for you:* Ask your friends, your family members, and the saints to pray for you and your prayer ministry.

Prayer Phase

Keep in mind these ten steps when you pray with others. Be prepared to adapt these based on culture, time constraints, and environment.

---

45 Fasting need not only be from food. One can fast from an activity or behavior as well, such as watching your favorite television show.

THE 10 STEPS

1. Initial Meeting
2. Ask Questions
3. Ask Permission
4. Invite the Presence and Offer Praise
5. Wait on the Spirit to Direct the Prayer
6. Pray in the Name of Jesus
7. Check for Results
8. Receive the Blessing of the Father
9. Seal the Prayer
10. Give Praise, Honor, and Glory to God

Step 1: Initial Meeting

Establish a relationship with the person for whom you will pray, and consider the environment. Discern: Are you in a safe place to pray? Is the place conducive to prayer? Do you have time to pray?

If there are multiple people praying for a person, have one act as the leader of the prayer. When praying on a prayer team that includes ordained persons, the one who holds the highest office should take on the position of leader. While there are some exceptions to this guideline, the one holding the highest office should assume leadership in the prayer team and, if necessary, be the one responsible for delegating an alternative leader.

The leader should make the initial introductions, such as, "Hi, it's nice to meet you. I'm glad you're here today. My name is ____;

*and this is ____ and ____. What is your name?" "Where are you
from?" "Have you ever been prayed for by someone?"*

Step 2: Ask Questions

Ask the individual what he or she would like the team to pray for
and if he or she is familiar with the Holy Spirit. Find out briefly
what the person's spiritual background is. Be on guard if you
suspect that the person has any associations with satanic practices or the occult, as well as the presence of any addictions or
compulsions.

> *"What would you like us to pray for?" "Have you ever been part
> of a prayer team before?" "What's your spiritual background?"
> "Tell us about your injury; how did that happen?" "Have you
> received any prayer or treatment for this yet?"*

Step 3: Ask Permission

Ask permission to pray for the individual and to lay hands on
him or her if you discern this would be helpful. If you feel your
gift of prayer tongues may be useful in helping you yield to
the Holy Spirit, ask permission from the person to use tongues
before you pray quietly in this manner. See general guidelines
in this session (2.4) for more information about the laying on of
hands and use of tongues.

> *"Would you mind if I prayed for you?" "Can I place my hand on
> your shoulder?" "Would you mind if I quietly pray in tongues?"*

Step 4: Invite the Presence and Offer Praise

Begin each of your prayer sessions by bringing about an awareness of the presence of God and giving praise to God. God is always present; he is always around us. When we pray, "Come, Holy Spirit," we are not asking a God who is far away to come near but rather awakening an awareness within ourselves of the presence of God already around us.

> "Come, Holy Spirit, come." "Jesus, we thank you and praise you for the gift of ____." "Lord, thank you for your goodness. You are holy; you are faithful."

Step 5: Wait on the Spirit to Direct the Prayer

We do not know how to pray as we ought (see Romans 8:26), and therefore it is important in prayer groups to give the Holy Spirit permission to lead the prayer. One way we can do this is by beginning the prayer session by asking God, "Tell us how we are to pray."

When we do this, we must be prepared for the most obvious next step: Wait for his response. Wait for a sense of the Spirit, and do not rush into the prayer. Avoid the temptation to pray in the flesh rather than in the Spirit.

Fr. Bob Hogan, in his article "Prayer Ministry for Evangelization," points out some common temptations to pray in the flesh:[46]

- We may respond too quickly to a perception and not wait

---

46   Hogan, Fr. Bob, Prayer Ministry for Evangelization. Catholic Charismatic Renewal
     Resources, 86-87.

for a prompting from the Holy Spirit. This might come from the desire to convey an immediate sense of love and concern for the person.

- A praying individual may feel "left out" if the others members of the group have "received" something from the Lord but the individual has not. The person may be tempted to make up something in the hope of fitting in.
- A praying person may so want to get an inspired "word" for someone that he or she shares something remembered from the past.
- A person praying may like the attention he or she gets from the person being prayed for.

"Jesus, how should we pray?" "Lord, tell us how we are to pray" "Lord, reveal to us how you desire us to pray" "Lord, tell us where to knock and what to ask."

Step 6: Pray in the Name of Jesus

After receiving direction from the Holy Spirit on how to pray, begin praying for the person. Maybe the person is led to repent of a sin, ask for forgiveness, or grant forgiveness. Maybe he or she is in bondage, and an evil spirit needs to be renounced. Whatever the prayer, the name of Jesus is powerful, and we are encouraged as Christians to pray in the name of Jesus. Pray expectantly for miracles.

"In the name of Jesus, receive healing." "Lord, I ask that you bless _____ with consolation in the name of Jesus." "Lord Jesus, remove from this person all influence of the enemy." "In the name of Jesus, grant _____ the graces to desire to forgive."

Step 7: Check for Results

After praying or sharing a word from the Holy Spirit, check on the person you are praying with. If you have prayed for healing, has the person received it? Can you test for it? Ask if he or she would like to continue praying.

Does the person look uncomfortable, bored, scared? Pay attention to what's going on, and try to adjust your prayer to honor the person. Look for and follow the fruits of the Holy Spirit.

"The source from whom every good gift comes is God, who is above all, blessed for ever. He who is all good has made all things good, so that he might fill his creatures with blessings and even after the Fall he has continued his blessings as a sign of his merciful love." —Book of Blessings, General Introduction, Paragraph 1

If you are praying for something specific and it is not coming (healing, understanding, consolation), ask God what the blocks may be. Repeat step 5, waiting on the Lord for his response. If you cannot find any good fruit from the prayer, ask God what do to, and again repeat step 5 or end the prayer.

"How are you doing?" "Can you tell me how you feel right now?" "Do you feel that God is doing anything within you right now?" "Would you like to continue praying?" "Are you comfortable trying to test for healing?"

Step 8: Receive the Blessing of the Father

When we pray with another person, he or she usually confesses sin, renounces a lie, or in prayers for healing, is freed of the sickness or injury. A void can exist where sin and death had previously taken hold of the person's heart. At the end of your prayer, ask Jesus to fill these voids with his blessing.

… When through the Church we ask for God's blessing, we should intensify our personal dispositions through faith, for which all things are possible; we should place our assurance in the hope that does not disappoint; above all we should be inspired by the love that impels us to keep God's commandments. Then, seeking what is pleasing to God, we will fully appreciate his blessing and will surely receive it.[47]

"In the name of Jesus, receive in abundance the Father's blessing." "Lord, enter into her heart and fill the voids with your blessing." "Jesus, where there was sin and regret, we ask that you replace and fill those places of her heart and soul with your love and blessing."

Step 9: Seal the Prayer

Seal the prayer for the person. Ask for God's mercy and blessing over the prayer session. If any doors to evil have been closed, ask that God seal them shut and send a guardian angel to stand and protect this door for all eternity. Ask God's blessing over the prayer, that he purify everything that was shared or said. If the individual is Catholic, encourage him or her to seal their prayer in the sacrament of penance and reconciliation.

"Jesus, we ask that for any doors that were closed tonight, you send a guardian angel to guard it for all eternity." "We seal this prayer in Jesus's name."

---

47   Book of Blessings, paragraph 15.

Step 10: Give Praise, Honor, and Glory to God

At the end of your prayer session, give praise to God. Thank him for his words, his consolations, his healings, and all that he has done.

> *"Lord, we praise you, we thank you, and we glorify you for your mighty love for us." "Jesus, thank you for listening and responding to our prayer."*

Post-Care Phase

It is important to always consider the heart of the person we have been praying with. Sometimes our prayers are answered immediately; other times, we may need follow-up care with other prayer ministries, a psychologist, or a counselor.

If the individual has revealed that he or she intends to harm self or another, let the person know that you *must* report this. Report it according to established diocesan safe-environment guidelines.

If the individual needs psychiatric care or counseling, gently recommend this. At Arise Worship Ministry events, we offer individuals a contact card with information to direct them to trained persons who have the faculties to help them.

If the individual needs follow-up prayer, it is permissible to offer a time for this. Share with the individual the contact card mentioned above and instruct the person to contact the ministry leader to schedule further prayer at a later time.

Signs Confirming Successful Intercessory Prayer

Though not an exhaustive list, the following signs are indications that your prayer was successful and fruitful:

- Good fruit appears: peace, patience, kindness, gentleness, unity.
- Healing occurs.
- The person experiences tears, resting in the Spirit, or a sense of peace.
- The person is brought into an encounter with Jesus Christ.
- The person is led closer to the sacraments or has a greater desire to receive the sacraments.
- Deliverance occurs.

Note that sometimes we are not granted the consolation of knowing our prayers were successful. If you are being granted consolation, the proper response is one of praise and thanksgiving.

Pastoral Care for Those Who Pray

While it is important to have a pastoral heart while praying for others, it is also good to be pastoral when on the receiving end of prayer.

In this course, many of your classmates are discerning and discovering the sound of the Spirit in their hearts. During this time, they may utter incomplete prophecies or non-prophecies. In these cases, consider their hearts as you urge them to grow. Use the language you would most like used with you.

> *"Thank you for that word, but it doesn't really resonate with me. Would you go back to the inspiration and see if you get a clearer picture?" "Thank you, but that word isn't bringing a sense of peace within me."*

Sometimes your classmates will bring with them bad prayer habits.

Maybe they become pushy, loud, and obnoxious, or their prayer may make you feel uncomfortable. Again, use this as an opportunity to help them grow.

> *"Thank you for praying for me; however, I was very distracted by your prayer tongue, and it prevented me from being able to focus." "I'm sorry, but the way you are praying for me makes me feel uncomfortable." "Remember, it is against the Arise prayer ministry guidelines to _____."*

We can gently encourage our brothers and sisters to continue to grow in and discern the voice of the Holy Spirit in their own lives without creating shame or embarrassment. It is in these environments, where individuals feel safe enough to practice and explore, that confidence will grow, discernment will happen, and prayer groups will mature.

◆ Reflect. Receive. Respond.

- Do you think that God is calling you to face-to-face intercessory prayer ministry? Why or why not?
- How can you prepare to be a part of an intercessory prayer team?
- Have you experienced trauma? Do you struggle with an addiction or compulsion? What steps can you take to overcome these obstacles to ministry?
- What tools can you use to help you remember the steps to prayer?
- What about intercessory prayer interests you? What excites you?
- What about intercessory prayer makes you nervous?

- How would you respond if someone on your prayer team became obnoxious or forceful during prayer?
- How would you respond if someone confided in you during your prayer session that he or she wanted to harm self or others?

2.4

GENERAL GUIDELINES FOR ARISE PRAYER TEAMS

With all prayer and supplication, pray at every opportunity in the Spirit. To that end, be watchful with all perseverance and supplication for all the holy ones. (Ephesians 6:18)

Below are some guidelines to keep in mind while working as part of an intercessory prayer team. While there is flexibility around certain guidelines, to pray as a representative of the Arise prayer ministry, these guidelines must be strictly adhered to:

1. **Sacraments:** The highest form of worship and the source and summit of the faith is the reception of the Eucharist. The goal of your prayers with others is to lead them into union with Christ and thus toward the sacramental life of the Church. Encourage those you pray with to receive the Eucharist, and

if they repent of any sin during the prayer session, encourage them to formally seek absolution in the sacrament of penance and reconciliation.

> *... The most intimate cooperation of the Holy Spirit and the Church is achieved in the liturgy. The Spirit, who is the Spirit of communion, abides indefectibly in the Church. For this reason the Church is the great sacrament of divine communion which gathers God's scattered children together. Communion with the Holy Trinity and fraternal communion are inseparably the fruit of the Spirit in the liturgy.*[48]

2. **Leadership:** In each prayer team, a leader should be appointed. Generally, this will be the person with the highest office in the Church. "[W]henever a priest or deacon is present, the office of presiding should be left to him."[49] This individual can choose to yield leadership to another person. For larger gatherings, a presider should be appointed as well.

3. **Watching:** Pray with your eyes open, and watch the person you are praying for so that you may discern what the Holy Spirit is doing.

4. **The Laying on of Hands:** Always ask permission to touch another person, and be very sensitive to your position and posture around him or her. Unless you have been granted an office of authority over the person, do not lay hands on the head. An

---

48   *CCC* 1108; see 1 John 1:3–7.

49   *Book of Blessings*, paragraph 18

exception to this is when you are praying for an injury or illness located on the head. Do not massage. Be careful to lay hands in a place that does not cause scandal. Avoid eccentricities. Be natural, not intense. Do not push, pull, or apply physical pressure. Also remember that while touching the person may be helpful, it is not always necessary.

5. *Praying Over vs. Praying With:* Continuing with the theme of authority and the spirit of humility, we ought to not pray with authority over anyone that God has not granted us authority over. Thus, in most prayer sessions, you will pray *for* or *with* another person.

6. *Communicating Words of Knowledge:* Maintaining a spirit of humility, offer any prophetic words in a manner that allows the individual to weigh and even reject them without embarrassment (see section 4.3 on prophecy). Do not say, "The Holy Spirit told me ___," or, "God says ___." Instead say, "This is what came to mind while we were praying," or "I sense ___; does that resonate with you?" During public ministry, do not give dates, mates, or directive prophecies.

7. *Being a Channel, Not a Storehouse:* In prayers for healing or deliverance, never take on the other person's suffering (for example, receiving their pain, illness, or oppression in exchange for their healing). You are a channel of God's grace to flow into others. You are not called to take on or receive their suffering or oppression. If you think this has happened, privately renounce it and speak to a prayer leader as soon as possible.

8. *Feedback and Review:* Throughout the prayer process, ask the individual questions. Do not be afraid to ask, "Do you feel God saying anything to you?" "How do you feel?" or, "Are you aware of God doing anything?" Adjust your prayer accordingly. Remember, you will know a work by its fruits. Constantly discern the fruit of the Holy Spirit. Look for the fruit in your prayer.

9. *Shame, Guilt, and Blame:* The Holy Spirit does not speak to his people through fear, doubt, insecurity, guilt, shame, or blame. Sometimes an individual may not be ready to deal with or face a serious sin. However, when the Spirit moves, he encourages rather than condemns. Be wary of negative emotions, as they are an indication that there is disorder in the prayer. "But the wisdom from above is first of all pure, then peaceable, gentle, compliant, full of mercy and good fruits, without inconstancy or insincerity" (James 3:17).

10. *Prudence:* Remain humble in your prayer, and do not go beyond the authority God has given you. Do not try to add to a prophecy or speak more than what the Holy Spirit has shared with you. Sometimes you must discern the proper time (if any) to share a word of knowledge. Some words are only for the prayer minister and not for the one who is being prayed for. Use common sense and practice prudence while discerning these things.

11. *Manifestations:* As a general guideline in Arise prayer ministry, if someone begins manifesting demonic influences (for example, thrashing, yelling, seizing), *stop the prayer.* If necessary, quietly and discreetly move the individual to a private setting.

If you are not properly formed or trained in deliverance ministry, do not attempt it. (Session 3 will cover deliverance prayer.)

12. *Uncertainty and Stopping Prayer:* Feel confident to *end* a prayer session if an individual begins manifesting in a negative way or if you feel uncomfortable or unsafe. If you are uncertain of how to pray effectively for a person, do not hesitate to seek advice from a team leader or refer the person to someone else.

13. *Accountability:* As often as possible, pray as part of a team of two or more, preferably with members of the same gender.

14. *Resting in the Spirit:* If you anticipate that someone may rest in the Spirit, do not try to push the person down. If the Lord desires him or her to rest in the Spirit, he will do it without your help.

    Have someone on the prayer team prepared to catch people in case they fall. Do not disturb a person who is resting in the Spirit, unless he or she has been resting for a long time. Try to avoid a "collection of bodies" at the front of a prayer service. Arise prayer ministry teams use small "modesty blankets" to cover from the torso down those resting in the Spirit.

    After resting in the Spirit in a public place, an individual might be confused and embarrassed, especially if it is the person's first time. In a pastoral spirit, have two individuals ready to pray and minister to the person.

15. *Perseverance:* When we pray, God always answers. Sometimes we do not recognize his answer, but that does not mean our prayer isn't efficacious. Persevere in prayer.

16. *The Use of Blessed Oil:* Out of respect for the office of the priesthood and to avoid confusion around the sacrament of Anointing of the Sick, members of Arise prayer ministry are not permitted to bless with oil.[50]

17. *Advising:* Practice prudence in advising someone after a prayer session. Never suggest that anyone stop using medicine or equipment that has been prescribed by a doctor. When giving advice, you may encourage a person to grow spiritually, forgive another, and avoid occasions of sin and occult practices.

18. *Prayer Service Leadership Team:* For large prayer meetings where there are many prayer teams, establish a leadership team to oversee the prayer ministry, keep order, and deal with any problems that may arise.

19. *Deliverance Prayers during Public Services:* During a *public* event at which many in the congregation are coming forward for healing, specific deliverance prayers are *not* permitted. You may quietly and calmly bind and renounce in Jesus's name anything that is not from the Lord (demonic influences); however, the prayer must stop at the first sign of a negative manifestation. (Session 3 will focus on deliverance prayer.) If the prayer session during a public service is in a private area, certain deliverance prayers are permitted, but again, must stop at the first sign of a negative manifestation.

---

50 See *Instruction on Certain Questions Regarding the Collaboration of the Non-Ordained Faithful in the Sacred Ministry of Priest* (Vatican City: Libreria Editrice Vaticana, 1997), art. 9, Vatican.va.

20. *Confidentiality:* You have a responsibility to keep confidential anything you learn in the course of praying for someone. If, however, it is revealed during the prayer session that the person intends to cause harm to self or another person, you have a responsibility to say to the person, "I cannot keep this a secret; I have to tell someone." Then you must report the incident to proper authorities.

21. *Personal Struggles of Prayer Team Members:* If you are presently struggling with an addiction or compulsion, or if you have recently experienced great trauma (loss of a loved one, serious illness or diagnosis), the Church has a responsibility to pray and care for *you.* Excuse yourself from leadership for the time being, and allow the Lord to come to you, offering you healing. If you are concerned about whether you may currently be in a position where you will need to step back from public prayer ministry, please consult a leader of your prayer ministry. It is critical that ministry leadership keep your story and situation entirely confidential. Strict confidentiality is the policy of Arise Worship Ministry.

22. *Tongues:* Be especially discerning with this gift. A personal prayer tongue is just that, personal. It is not meant for the public assembly. However, sometimes praying in a prayer tongue may help the intercessor yield more obediently to the Holy Spirit.

    If you do not know the individual you are praying with, and thus are not sure of the person's response to tongues, *ask permission* to pray in tongues. Be pastoral, and explain the gift before you begin. If you choose to pray in tongues, you must

do so quietly, not drawing attention to yourself or becoming a
distraction to the prayer.

23. *Peaceful Assembly:* At all times, a sense of peace and calm
     must be maintained during the prayer session. Never yell,
     command, shout, or raise your voice during a prayer session.
     Power does not come from how loudly or forcefully you pray;
     power comes from the Spirit. Avoid anything resembling
     theatrics, hysteria, sensationalism, or artificiality.

24. *Reporting:* "Those who direct healing services ... are ... to
     exercise the necessary prudence if healings should take
     place among those present; when the celebration is over, any
     testimony can be collected with honesty and accuracy, and
     submitted to the proper ecclesiastical authority."[51]

25. *Lying and Withholding:* In some cases, the Holy Spirit may
     grant you an insight or word, and when you ask the person
     for feedback, he or she may lie to you or withhold information.
     These times can be very discouraging to intercessors because
     they bring doubt and confusion, especially regarding the dis-
     cernment of one's spiritual gifts. It is good to remember in these
     moments that intercessory prayer is not for yourself but for the
     other. While the individual may choose to reject your insight
     or lie to you, your obligation and duty is to remain in a spirit
     of service and humility. Entrust your moments of doubt and
     confusion to God, and allow the Lord to heal and bring peace.

---

51   Congregation for the Doctrine of the Faith, *Instruction on Prayers for Healing* (Vatican
     City: Holy See, September 14, 2000), art 9, Vatican.va.

26. ***Concluding the Prayer:*** Always assure the individual of the Father's love for him or her, regardless of any outcome. There is no need to be disappointed if the desired outcome is not immediately present. Answers to prayer can be gradual. Always encourage the person to receive more prayer, read the Scriptures, and receive the sacraments. When appropriate, offer the individual information on opportunities to receive follow-up care.

◆ Reflect. Receive. Respond.

- Which of these guidelines surprise you?
- How would you respond if you witnessed someone on your ministry team not adhering to these guidelines?
- Is there a guideline you think should be added?

practicum

FOR SESSION 2

exercise 1

GROUP DISCUSSION: HEALING OF THE EYE

Directions

Read the following story and answer the reflection questions.

A young teacher, Cathy, was at a conference when she noticed a volunteer with a wet paper towel over her eye. "Oh, my goodness, what happened to your eye?" Cathy asked.

"I don't know," said the volunteer. "When I woke up this morning, I was in a great deal of pain. My eye is rough and scratchy, and it hurts to blink. When people look at it, the eye looks fine. But it hurts, and it's been getting worse all day."

"Have you taken anything for it?" Cathy asked.

"Yes, I put some eye drops in, but nothing really seems to help it."

"Aw, man, I am so sorry."

As Cathy started to walk away, it occurred to her that she could offer to pray for this stranger. Unsure if this was the right thing to do, she turned around and asked, "Hey, has anyone offered to pray for your eye yet?"

The woman looked surprised, "No, why?"

"I hope it doesn't sound strange, but if you'd like, we could try praying for your eye and see if God may heal it."

To Cathy's surprise, the woman was receptive. "I think that would be great!"

"Awesome. What's your name? Mine's Cathy."

"I'm Jennifer."

"Nice to meet you. Would you mind if I put my hand near your eye?"

"No, not at all."

"OK, let's pray." Cathy and Jennifer moved to a quiet space a few steps over, and Cathy began to pray, "Come, Holy Spirit, come. Jesus, we invite your presence in. Lord, show us how we are to pray."

Cathy waited for a few moments before continuing. "Jesus, I ask that you come and bring healing to Jennifer's eye. Jesus, take away her pain and discomfort, and replace it with healing, blessing, comfort, and consolation. In the name of Jesus, receive healing."

Cathy looked at Jennifer, whose body continued to relax through the prayer. Consoled by this positive interaction, Cathy decided to keep praying. After a moment of silence, Cathy began to imagine an eye seeing painful things. As she focused on this image, she began to pray,

"Jesus, I ask that you heal the memories of anything Jennifer may have seen—in a dream, in person, in a vision, anything that she may have seen that has caused her harm, pain, or anxiety. In your name, I pray that you cleanse what her eye has seen and bring healing."

Jennifer, whose eyes were closed, nodded as if in agreement with the prayer.

Cathy began to feel as if the prayer was over. She checked with Jennifer, "How do you feel?"

Jennifer started to blink and test her eye. "Well, I feel really peaceful, and my eye feels better, but it's not 100 percent better."

"So it's not 100 percent, but it feels better?"

"Oh, yeah, it's much better. Wow. Yes, it does feel better. Just not 100 percent. It still hurts a little, but not nearly as much as before."

"Well, praise God. I'm really consoled that it's feeling better. I wonder if this healing may slowly seep in, like a fine oil or a slow-release ibuprofen tablet. If it continues to improve, will you let me know?"

"Yes, absolutely."

Cathy and Jennifer bowed their heads once again as Cathy prayed, "Lord, we thank you. We praise you for your goodness. You are faithful. You are good. You are healer. We thank you for listening and responding. All glory be to you, Lord Jesus." The two embraced and departed in different directions.

Three hours later, Cathy was walking into a meeting room when she saw Jennifer running toward her.

"It's all better! My eye feels great! I think I've been healed! Thank you for your prayers!"

Cathy gave Jennifer a hug. "God is so good! How amazing. Thank you for sharing this with me."

"Yeah, after we prayed, it just kept getting better and better, and now all the pain is gone!"

◆ Reflect. Receive. Respond.

- Initially, Cathy was nervous about praying for Jennifer. Have you ever felt uncomfortable praying for a stranger? How did you handle that discomfort?
- What things do you like about Cathy's approach to this prayer session?
- What things could Cathy have done differently? What rules did she not follow?
- How would Cathy's actions change if Jennifer were an adult male? a young child?
- We learn in this story that sometimes healings are not immediate. How would you share this with someone you were praying with?

exercise 2

INTERCESSORY PRAYER TEAM

Directions

Break up into groups of three or more.

Spend five minutes individually preparing yourself for the prayer session. Discern if your spirit is in a place to be an active intercessor. If it is not, only offer simple prayers of blessing, praise, and thanksgiving throughout the exercise.

Bring the small group together. *Have one person come forward to receive prayer.* Follow the ten steps of prayer as an intercessory team.

When the prayer is over, *discuss the successes and failures of the prayer session.* What would you do differently next time? How did the person receiving prayer feel? How did the persons praying feel? Be honest in your discussion.

Repeat until all group members have received prayer. Pick one lesson or story that you and your group are willing to share with the group at large.

Share and discuss with the larger group.

Notes:

_____

_____

_____

_____

_____

_____

_____

session 3

DELIVERANCE PRAYER

3.1

THE CURÉ OF ARS

Then Jesus was led by the Spirit into the desert to be tempted by the devil. (Matthew 4:1)

"The Scriptures tell us that Satan at times disguises himself as an angel of light. In our days he is even more cunning: he persuades people, all too successfully, that he does not exist at all. One of the most amazing features of the life of the Curé of Ars is that during a period of about thirty-five years he was frequently molested, in a physical and tangible way, by the evil one.

It should be borne in mind that all men are subject to temptation—for to tempt to sin is the devil's "ordinary" occupation, so to speak—and temptation is permitted by God for our good. "Infestation" is an "extraordinary action" of the devil, when he seeks to terrify by horrible apparitions or noises. "Obsession" goes further: it is either "external," when the devil acts on the external senses of the body; or "internal," when he influences the imagination or the

memory. "Possession" occurs when the devil seizes on and uses
the whole organism. But even then mind and will remain out of
his reach. Most of the Curé of Ars's experiences belong to the first
category, viz., "infestation." …

… M. Vianney soon perceived that these displays of satanic
humour were fiercest when some great conversion was about to take
place, or, as he playfully put it, when he was about to "land a big
fish." One morning the devil set fire to his bed. The Saint had just
left his Confessional to vest for Mass when the cry, "Fire! fire!" was
raised. He merely handed the key of his room to those who were to
put out the flames: "The villainous grappin!" (it was his nickname
for the devil) "unable to catch the bird, he sets fire to the cage!" was
the only comment he made. To this day the pilgrim may see, hard
by the head of the bed, a picture with its glass splintered by the heat
of the flames. It must be remembered that at no time was a fire lit in
the hearth and there were no matches in the presbytery.

These molestations were both terrifying and ludicrous…. The
devil would go on for hours producing a noise similar to that made
by striking a glass tumbler with the blade of a steel knife; or he would
sing, "with a very cracked voice," the Saint said, or whistle for hours on
end; or he would produce a noise as of a horse champing and prancing
in the room, so that the wonder was that the worm-eaten floor did not
give way; or he would bleat like a sheep, or miaow like a cat, or shout
under the Curé's window: "Vianney! Vianney! potato-eater."

The purpose of these horrible or grotesque performances was to
prevent the servant of God from getting that minimum of rest which
his poor body required and thus to render him physically unfit to go on
with his astonishing work in the confessional by which he snatched so
many souls from the clutches of the fiend….

... Nevertheless, horrible as may be the condition of one whose body is possessed by the devil, it is as nothing by comparison with the wretched plight of a soul which, by mortal sin, sells itself, as it were, to Satan. The holy priest may be said to have spent the best part of his priestly career in a direct contest with sin through his unparalleled work in the confessional. The Curé's confessional was the real miracle of Ars, one that was not merely a passing wonder, or the sensation of a few weeks.... The astonishing thing about M. Vianney is that he himself personally became the object of a pilgrimage, people flocking to Ars in hundreds of thousands just to get a glimpse of him, to hear him, to exchange but a few words with him, above all, to go to confession to him. [52]

◊ Reflect. Receive. Respond.

- Why did Satan want to harass St. John Vianney?
- What was the real miracle of Ars?
- When was the last time you made a good confession?

---

52   Abbé François Trochu, *The Curé d'Ars: St. Jean-Marie-Baptiste Vianney*, trans. Ernest Graf (London: Incorporated Catholic Truth Society, 1952), www.ewtn.com.

3.2

AN INTRODUCTION TO DELIVERANCE

These signs will accompany those who believe: in my name they will drive out demons, they will speak new languages. (Mark 16:17)

> *The existence of Satan ("the Devil") and other malevolent spirits (demons, "fallen angels") is an integral part of the teaching of the Catholic Church....[53]*

> *Satan or the devil and the other demons are fallen angels who have freely refused to serve God and his plan. Their choice against God is definitive. They try to associate man in their revolt against God.[54]*

---

53   Rev. Dr. Gareth Leyshon, *Exorcism and Prayers for Deliverance: The Position of the Catholic Church*, version 2 (Cardiff, Wales: Cardiff, 2016), p. 4.

54   *CCC* 414.

Satan is first introduced to Christians at the beginning of Sacred
Scripture. In the Book of Genesis, one reads the story of how Satan,
appearing as a serpent, tempted Eve to bite the fruit from the tree
of Knowledge of Good and Evil (see Genesis 3:6), an act implicitly
forbidden by God (see Genesis 3:3).

> *Behind the disobedient choice of our first parents lurks a seductive*
> *voice, opposed to God, which makes them fall into death out of*
> *envy [see Genesis 3:1-5; Wisdom 2:24]. Scripture and the Church's*
> *Tradition see in this being a fallen angel, called "Satan" or the "devil"*
> *[John 8:44; Revelation 12:9]. The Church teaches that Satan was at*
> *first a good angel, made by God: "The devil and the other demons*
> *were indeed created naturally good by God, but they became evil by*
> *their own doing."*[55]

The consequences of our first parents' disobedience were grave.
Both Adam and Eve were exiled from their first home, the Garden
of Eden. Further consequences included labor pains, difficulties
in toil, and eventual death. (see Genesis 3:16–19). The *Catechism*
teaches that, after this first sin, the world was "virtually inundated
by sin."[56] Fr. Gabriele Amorth, author of *An Exorcist Tells His Story*,
concurs: "By means of his [Satan's] temptation, evil, pain, sin, and
death entered the world."[57]

In this one action, the keys to the kingdom of the earth were
exchanged. Through sin, Adam and Eve renounced the power and

---

55   *CCC* 391, quoting Lateran Council IV (1215): DS 800.

56   *CCC* 401.

57   Gabriele Amorth, *An Exorcist Tells His Story* (San Francisco: Ignatius, 1999), p. 21.

authority over the earth that God had given them, and Satan took
their place and became prince of this world (see CCC 409; 2 Corinthians 4:4; Ephesians 2:2). All hope would seem lost, except God,
never tiring in his great love for us, predestined Jesus Christ to
come to earth as Savior and Redeemer.

> *After his fall, man was not abandoned by God. On the contrary,
> God calls him and in a mysterious way heralds the coming
> victory over evil and his restoration from his fall [see Genesis 3:9,
> 15]. This passage in Genesis is called the* Protoevangelium *("first
> gospel"): the first announcement of the Messiah and Redeemer,
> of a battle between the serpent and the Woman, and of the final
> victory of a descendant of hers.*[58]

Christ's saving work on the cross merited for us the grace for our
sins to be forgiven. Because of Christ's death on the cross, the gates
of heaven were once again opened for us. And also, by his death and
resurrection, Christ broke the power of the evil one and took back
authority over this world.

> *Christians believe that "the world has been established and
> kept in being by the Creator's love; has fallen into slavery to sin
> but has been set free by Christ, crucified and risen to break the
> power of the evil one...."*[59]

---

58   CCC 410.

59   CCC 421, quoting Vatican II, *Gaudium et Spes*, 2 §2.

In the New Testament, Christ repeatedly delivers individuals of demonic influence (see Mark 1:34; 16:9; Luke 11:14). Christ commissioned his apostles to imitate him in this great work: "Go into the whole world and proclaim the gospel to every creature.... These signs will accompany those who believe: In my name they will drive out demons" (Mark 16:15, 17). We know that the disciples did this because, when the seventy-two returned to Christ, they said, "Lord, even the demons are subject to us because of your name" (Luke 10:17).

After Christ's ascension into heaven, the disciples carried on this important work of taking authority over evil in Jesus's name. Early Christian writers like Tertullian and Origen teach us that, in the first and second centuries, the practice of exorcism was widely used. There are even notes indicating that some of the practitioners, rather than being priests, were some of the simplest and rudest of the faithful.[60]

This general freedom in the practice of exorcism was short-lived. Very quickly the Church began instituting safeguards around the practice of exorcism. At the Fourth Council of Carthage in AD 398, the Church introduced the first rite of ordination for exorcists. By this point, the practice of exorcism was limited to ordained priests. In this original rite, the bishop was to give the priest a book containing the formulae of exorcism, and then the bishop would encourage the priest to commit the entire prayer to memory.

Throughout the centuries, the Church would occasionally write certain orders regarding further safeguards for exorcism prayer. Such safeguards included the rule that only priests could practice exorcism, a priest had to have the permission of his local

---

60   See Origen, *Against Celsus*, bk. VII, chap. 4.

ordinary, and exorcisms could not take place during the adoration of the Blessed Sacrament.

With the advent of the Catholic Charismatic Renewal in 1967, there has been renewed interest among the laity in the ministry of deliverance. "In the absence of authoritative Church guidance, and following the example of Pentecostal Churches, there has been unrestricted experimentation by Catholics … in the 'ministry of deliverance' which seeks to bring relief to those afflicted by demonic spirits."[61]

To address this problem, session 3 will provide (1) clarification on the definitions and vocabulary used in exorcism and deliverance ministry and (2) general norms and guidelines specific to lay persons who may be involved in deliverance ministry.

◆ Reflect. Receive. Respond.

- Do you believe in the devil? Who is he?
- Have you ever witnessed someone do deliverance ministry? What was your impression?
- Has anyone ever prayed for you to experience deliverance or exorcism? Describe your experience.

---

61   Leyshon, p. 2.

3.3

DEFINITIONS

A thief comes only to steal and slaughter and destroy; I came so that they might have life and have it more abundantly. (John 10:10)

Before we can move into a teaching and discussion on deliverance, a standard vocabulary and understanding of terms must be established.

Demonization and Its Types

Demonization is any instances in which a person, place, or thing is subject to the influence of demons. This includes infestation, oppression, obsession, and possession. The following definitions have been compiled by Rev. Dr. Gareth Leyshon from the archdiocese of Cardiff:

Infestation is used to refer to the influence of evil spirits over objects, animals, houses or places. These can become infested by exposure to occult activity or by a deliberate curse being directed towards them.[62]

Oppression: demonic influence which seems to come from outside a person, causing heaviness, weariness or discouragement. Oppressive spirits may be acquired through exposure to a heavy presence of evil: e.g. by participating in deliverance ministry ..., by coming into contact with items of witchcraft. Oppressive spirits may be dispelled by a simple command to leave in the name of Jesus.[63]

Obsession:[64] demonic influence which seems to reside inside a person, usually afflicting a certain area in a person's life in the form of strong habitual temptations. A person may open oneself to such influence by deliberately seeking the presence or power of evil spirits through witchcraft, Satanism, or fortune-telling (Ouija, tarot, etc.); demonic obsession may also occur through other grave sins which are not explicitly associated with the occult, e.g. sexual activity by consecrated or ordained persons pledged to celibacy. The obsessing spirit usually needs to be identified by name and cast out (i.e. commanded to leave) or bound (i.e. forbidden from exerting any further influence). [65]

Possession: The rarest of demonic attack, possession "occurs when human beings willfully hand over complete control of their life to Satan, by expressly doing so or by embracing grave sin. Formal exorcism, sanctioned by the diocesan bishop, is always required in such cases....

---

62   Leyshon, p. 4.
63   Leyshon, p. 4.
64   *Obsession* here is not to be confused with an intense interest or curiosity with someone or something, which is also termed an obsession.
65   Leyshon, p. 4.

[Possession] is characterized by spectacular features in which the demon takes control, in a certain manner, of the strength and physical abilities of the person possessed. It cannot, however, take over the free will of the subject, so the demon cannot force the person possessed to choose to sin.... [66]

Other terms that must be clearly defined and differentiated are *exorcism* and *deliverance*, and the spoken formulas for both.

Exorcism

According to the *Catholic Encyclopedia*: "**Exorcism** is (1) the act of driving out, or warding off, demons, or evil spirits, from persons, places, or things, which are believed to be possessed or infested by them, or are liable to become victims or

> "All faiths, all cultures, have exorcists, but only Christianity has the true force to exorcise through Christ's example and authority." —Fr. Gabriele Amorth, *Sunday Telegraph interview*

instruments of their malice; (2) the means employed for this purpose, especially the solemn and authoritative adjuration of the demon, in the name of God, or any of the higher power in which he is subject." [67]

The Church divides exorcism into two categories: minor exorcism and major exorcism.

Minor exorcism is common to every Catholic, because every Catholic has received at least one. "The Church's rites of Baptism for Adults and

---

66 Leyshon, pp. 4, 12.

67 Patrick Toner, "Exorcism," in *Catholic Encyclopedia*, vol. 5 (New York: Robert Appleton, 1909), newadvent.org.

Children include prayers called **minor exorcisms.**[68] These minor exorcisms can be offered even when "there is no need for evidence that the catechumen is not being specifically afflicted by demons." [69]

"For a demon to leave a body and go back to hell means to die forever and to lose any ability to molest people in the future. He expresses his desperation saying: 'I am dying, I am dying. You are killing me; you have won. All priests are murderers.'"

—Fr. Gabriele Amorth, interview

For the most part, lay persons are restricted from performing minor exorcisms; however, the Second Vatican Council's *Sacrosanctum Concilium* allows for lay catechists, deputed by their local bishop, to confer the minor exorcism as part of the Rite of Christian Initiation of Adults. The lay catechist may not perform a minor exorcism outside of this approved rite.[70]

The second term, **major exorcism**, refers to the Rite of Exorcism reserved for persons who are possessed.

Before performing a **major exorcism**, the priest-exorcist must be very sure that the person is, in fact, possessed rather than suffering from mental illness. Certain signs often accompany an individual who is possessed, including "speaking or understanding many words of unlearned languages; disclosing things at a distance or hidden; exerting strength beyond the possessed person's natural ability; and these together with vehement aversion to God, the Virgin Mary, the Saints, the cross and holy images."[71]

---

68   Leyshon, p. 5.

69   Leyshon, p. 5.

70   In very rare and extreme circumstances, *in extremis* and as a damage-limitation method, a lay person may pray for the exorcism of another. It is unlikely that any participant in this course will be in this situation. More on this topic can be found in the section 3.7, "General Guidelines for Deliverance Ministry."

71   Cardinal Medina Estevez, speaking on the release of the 1999 *De Exorcismis et Supplicationibus Quibusdam*, Rite of Exorcism.

Once possession has been determined, the major exorcism can only be performed by a priest-exorcist, who has also been granted permission by his bishop or ordinary, to perform the major exorcism. Lay persons are not permitted to perform a major exorcism.

Deliverance

As lay persons are restricted from performing major exorcisms and the practice of minor exorcism is limited for use only to deputed catechesis within the Rite of Christian Initiation for Adults, the majority of this session will cover *deliverance ministry*, which is open to lay persons. Deliverance is "a generic term for freeing someone from the influence of a demon, is applied specifically to cases of obsession and oppression of persons, and infestation of places."[72]

Deprecative vs. Imperative Formula

There are two spoken formulas in deliverance ministry:

> **Deprecative formula** is "a prayer which petitions God to liberate a person from the influence of an evil spirit."[73] For example, *"Lord Jesus, remove from this person any evil spirit."*

> **Imperative formula** is "a command addressed directly to an evil spirit."[74] For example, *"In the name of Jesus, be gone, Satan!"*

---

72   Leyshon, p. 5.

73   Leyshon, p. 5.

74   Leyshon, p. 5.

Words have power, and Scripture repeatedly warns us of the power of the spoken word (see Proverbs 18:21; Matthew 12:36–37). This truth affects deliverance ministry as well. How we pray and what we pray matters.

The imperative formula is direct and very serious. The minor exorcism at baptism does not include the imperative formula but the more passive deprecative formula. The Vatican letter *Of Exorcisms and Certain Supplications* mandates that even in a case of major exorcism, the deprecative formula must precede the use of the imperative formula.[75]

This action of the Church preferring the deprecative formula is evidence which points to the gravity and seriousness with which the Church approaches the language used in deliverance and exorcism ministry.

◊ Reflect. Receive. Respond.

- What is the difference between infestation, oppression, obsession, and possession?
- What prayers have you learned that involve the deprecative formula for deliverance? (Hint: you say at least one at every Mass)

---

75   De Exorcismis et *Supplicationibus Quibusdam* (Vatican City: Libreria Editrice Vaticana, 1999).

3.4

DOORS TO DEMONIZATION

Be sober and vigilant. Your opponent the devil is prowling around like a roaring lion looking for [someone] to devour. Resist him, steadfast in faith, knowing that your fellow believers throughout the world undergo the same sufferings. (1 Peter 5:8–9)

When faced with an individual needing liberation from demonic influence, one may wonder, "Where did the evil come from?" and "Why are some people attacked more than others?"

The devil does not sleep. He constantly searches for ways to come into our hearts and minds. Scripture warns us to remain sober and alert to the potential onslaughts of the enemy (see 1 Peter 5:8–9). However, extreme manifestations of the enemy are rare. "The ordinary work of the Devil is temptation," says Bishop Thomas Paprocki, chairman of the Bishops'

"Walk with the wise and you become wise, but the companion of fools fares badly." —Proverbs 13:20

Committee on Canonical Affairs and Church Governance.[76] "The greatest trick of the devil is convincing you he doesn't exist," wrote Charles Baudelaire. Most often, the work of the devil is so subtle that it goes unnoticed.

So how do people find themselves under more extreme forms of spiritual attack?

The short answer is sin. Wherever there is sin in our lives, there is a door in our hearts that is opposed to God, and open to the enemy. Whenever we take agreement with a lie, refuse forgiveness, or commit other sins, we allow the enemy ground and entrance into our lives. Yet not all sin is created equal (see CCC 1852–1854). Certain sins render a soul more vulnerable to demonic influence or attack.

The Occult

One way the enemy enters into our lives and the lives of those we love is through the **occult**. What makes the sin of participation in the occult different from running a red light or lying on your tax return is that occult activity calls upon, and invites in, the spirits opposed to God. Scripture is very clear in forbidding and condemning its use:

> "The ordinary work of the Devil is temptation, and the ordinary response is a good spiritual life, observing the sacraments and praying. The Devil doesn't normally possess someone who is leading a good spiritual life."
> —Bishop Paprocki

Let there not be found among you anyone who causes their son or daughter to pass through the fire, or practices divination, or is a soothsayer, augur, or sorcerer, or who casts spells, consults ghosts

---

76   Bishop Thomas Paprocki, as quoted in Laurie Goodstein, "For Catholics, Interest in Exorcism Is Revived," *New York Times*, November 12, 2010, nytimes.com.

and spirits, or seeks oracles from the dead. Anyone who does such things is an abomination to the LORD. (Deuteronomy 18:10–12)

When we enter into occult practice, we enter into Satan's playground. At first, the occult may appear attractive because it appeals to the natural desire to know and encounter a supernatural power (God); however, the supernatural experiences found in occult practices are disordered, confusing, and dangerous. "This confusion begins when we recognize that there are other spiritual forces besides God and when we use them, attempt to consult them, or are preoccupied with staying on their 'good side.'"[77]

> *"Be angry but do not sin; do not let the sun set on your anger, and do not leave room for the devil."*
> —Ephesians 4:26-27

All forms of divination are to be rejected: recourse to Satan or demons, conjuring up the dead or other practices falsely supposed to "unveil" the future [see Deuteronomy 18:10; Jeremiah 29:8]. Consulting horoscopes, astrology, palm reading, interpretation of omens and lots, the phenomena of clairvoyance, and recourse to mediums all conceal a desire for power over time, history, and, in the last analysis, other human beings, as well as a wish to conciliate hidden powers. They contradict the honor, respect, and loving fear that we owe to God alone.[78]

> *"Whether we realize it or not, whether we are aware of it or not, whether we do it for fun, for amusement or for any other reason, it does not change anything: the devastating impact of spiritism is the same."* —Dr. Valter Cascioli, Association of Exorcists

---

77 Francis MacNutt, "Renouncing Occult Involvement," in *School of Healing Prayer* (Jacksonville, Fl.: Christian Healing Ministries, 1998).
78 CCC 2116.

To be explicit, the following, are considered occult activities:

- Visited a fortune teller or psychic or contacted a psychic hotline
- Read or followed horoscopes or had a chart made for oneself
- Practiced certain forms of eastern transcendental meditation
- Believing in reincarnation or had reincarnation reading
- Played with a Ouija board, tarot cards, or crystal ball
- Played games of an occult nature: using ESP or telepathy, calling upon spirits
- Consulted a medium, spiritualist, or numerologist
- Acted as a medium or practiced channeling
- Sought healing through magic spells or charms
- Practiced table lifting, levitation of objects, pendulum swinging, lifting of bodies, automatic writing, or soul travel
- Attended or participated in satanic worship services
- Worshiped at a shrine or temple of a non-Judeo/Christian religion (such as a Buddhist or Hindu temple)
- Practiced sorcery, magic arts, black magic, white magic, witchcraft, voodoo, or hoodoo
- Adherence to freemasonry
- Attended a séance or occult meeting

If you have experienced any of these activities, it is important to quickly bring this experience to a priest in the sacrament of confession and renounce your association with the occult. While exorcism expels demons from the body, confession expels them from the soul.

Grave Sin

Corresponding with the hierarchy of sin, **grave sin** (or mortal sin) makes us vulnerable to demonic attack because of its great offense against charity in the heart.[79] What makes a sin grave is specified by the Ten Commandments: "You know the commandments: 'You shall not kill; you shall not commit adultery; you shall not steal; you shall not bear false witness; you shall not defraud; honor your father and mother'" (Mark 10:19).

> "Christ ransomed us from the curse of the law by becoming a curse for us, for it is written, "Cursed be everyone who hangs on a tree," that the blessing of Abraham might be extended to the Gentiles through Christ Jesus, so that we might receive the promise of the Spirit through faith." —Galatians 3:13-14

When one commits one of these with full knowledge and full consent of the will, the individual is committing **mortal sin**. Grave sins could include (but are not limited to):

- drug use, alcohol abuse
- idol worship
- sexual immorality[80]
- abortion and other forms of murder
- the capital sins— pride, avarice, envy, wrath, lust, gluttony, and acedia[81]

Mortal sin "results in the loss of charity and the privation of sanctifying grace, that is, of the state of grace. If it is not redeemed by repentance and God's forgiveness, it causes exclusion from Christ's kingdom and the eternal death of hell, for our freedom has the power to make choices for ever, with no turning back."[82]

---

79   See *CCC* 1850, 1853, 1855.
80   Sexual immorality includes pornography, masturbation, prostitution, bestiality, group sex, infidelity, and other sexual deviance.
81   *CCC* 1866.
82   *CCC* 1861.

Curses

Just as a person may be given a blessed item or receive a blessing from someone, a person may also possess a cursed object or be cursed by another. In the Book of Deuteronomy, we read about the curse that befalls the person who brings a cursed object (in this case, an idol) into the home (see Deuteronomy 7:26). Jesus cursed the fig tree (Matthew 21:18–22), and Noah cursed his son Ham (Genesis 9:18–27).

◖ Reflect. Receive. Respond.

- Have you ever dabbled in the occult? Have you properly confessed it?
- How would you tell someone you love about the dangers of occult activity and grave sin?

3.5

DELIVERANCE PRAYER

The righteous cry out, the LORD hears and he rescues them from all their afflictions. (Psalm 34:18)

If you think that you, or someone you love may benefit from deliverance prayer ministry both your faith and your obedience to the Church's teachings on the practice of deliverance will help ensure the safe and successful practice of the ministry. Rather than relying on the precise use of an unchanging formula or a particular sequence of events, the success of deliverance or exorcism prayer "depends on two elements: authorization from valid and licit Church authorities, and the faith of the exorcist."[83] **Obedience** and **faith** are the two requirements for prayer ministry.

> *"But the Lord is faithful; he will strengthen you and guard you from the evil one." —2 Thessalonians 3:3*

---

83   Malacahi Martin, *Hostage to the Devil: The Possession and Exorcism of Five Contemporary Americans* (San Francisco: Harper, 1976), p. 459.

Considering the many safeguards in place, how can a lay person obediently practice this ministry?

Neal Lozano is one of the leading Catholic teachers on deliverance ministry. His book *Resisting the Devil: A Catholic Perspective on Deliverance* (Our Sunday Visitor, 2010) received an imprimatur from Bishop John D'Arcy of South Bend. While not official Church teaching, the following model uses Lozano's prescription for deliverance prayer and does not violate teachings from the Church regarding deliverance ministry.

> *"So submit yourselves to God. Resist the devil, and he will flee from you." —James 4:7*

Please note, for official Arise prayer teams, prayer team members are not permitted to pray the imperative formula over another individual.

Step 1: Repent

Peter famously said, "Repent and be baptized, every one of you, in the name of Jesus Christ for the forgiveness of your sins" (Acts 2:38). It is through sin that the demonic enters into our world, and thus it is through repentance and accepting God's forgiveness that a person begins to experience deliverance.

The person seeking deliverance should examine his or her conscience (the use of an examination of conscience worksheet is often helpful) and write down sins. For Catholics, it is ultimately important to take these repented sins into the confessional.

> **If praying for oneself:** *"In the name of Jesus, I repent of ___."*
> **If praying with others**, ask *"Will you say, 'In the name of Jesus, I repent of ___.'"* Or ask, *"Are there any sins you could repent of?"*

Step 2: Forgive

The Scriptures are very clear that we are not to hold grudges but rather forgive: "All bitterness, fury, anger, shouting, and reviling must be removed from you, along with all malice. [And] be kind to one another, compassionate, forgiving one another as God has forgiven you in Christ" (Ephesians 4:31–32). Choosing to forgive or not to forgive has consequences. "If you forgive others their transgressions, your heavenly Father will forgive you. But if you do not forgive others, neither will your Father forgive your transgressions" (Matthew 6:14–15).

The second step in deliverance prayer is offering forgiveness. The person being prayed with needs to ask God to reveal whom he or she needs to forgive. If the person cannot forgive, he or she can pray for the graces to desire to forgive. Lack of forgiveness can sometimes be the block that prevents our souls from receiving the deliverance we so long for.

> **If praying for oneself:** *"In the name of Jesus, I forgive ___ for ___."*
> Or, *"Jesus, grant me the graces to desire to forgive ___ for ___."*
> **If praying with others:** *"Is there anyone you need to forgive?"*

Step 3: Renounce

After both repenting of sin and forgiving, the individual is ready to renounce the spirit or spirits that have gained ground or influence.

Before beginning this prayer, one must consider the power of words. What we say has power. One of the most powerful words we will use in deliverance ministry is the name of Jesus. Fr. Gabriele Amorth shares his experience as an exorcist:

Christ's centrality tells us that we can be saved only in his name. It is only in his name that we can win and free ourselves from the enemy of our salvation, Satan. At the end of the most difficult exorcisms, when I am confronted with total demonic possession, I pray the Christological hymn of the Letter of Paul to the Philippians (2:6–11). When I speak the words "so that all beings in the heavens, on earth, and in the underworld should bend the knee at the name of Jesus," I kneel, everyone present kneels, and always the one possessed by the demons is also compelled to kneel. It is a moving and powerful moment.[84]

Other words are important to note. For example, the word *rebuke*. To **rebuke** is to express sharp disapproval or criticism. This word can sometimes bring to mind the image of a person screaming, *"I rebuke you in the name of Jesus!"* In this scenario, a good question to ask that individual is, "Do you mean what you are saying?"

Consider St. Michael the archangel in the Book of Jude:

Yet the archangel Michael, when he argued with the devil in a dispute over the body of Moses, did not venture to pronounce a reviling judgment upon him but said, "May the Lord rebuke you!" (Jude 9)

To rebuke something doesn't mean to send it away or demand it to leave. To rebuke the devil is to scold him. The archangel Michael refused to do this, so what makes us think that this is proper?

---

84   Amorth, p. 23.

What we really desire to do is *renounce* an evil spirit. To **renounce** is to formally declare one's abandonment of something or someone.

When we renounce a spirit by saying, *"In Jesus's name, I renounce the spirit of ___ "*, we aren't using the imperative formula, but the more appropriate deprecative. It's also what we really mean. We really do desire to renounce our attachment to evil. Through sin, we have given Satan power. By renouncing him, after repenting and forgiving, we break our ties with Satan and receive back that which was taken from us.

Another positive word is *bind*. To **bind** means "to tie, fasten, or constrain." When we renounce a spirit, it must leave, but some spirits may leave noisily, to try to instill fear in us. By praying that the spirit be bound in Jesus's name, we are asking Jesus "to tie" the spirit and prevent it from speaking, manifesting, or doing any further damage or harm.

When praying over oneself: *"Jesus, I ask that you bind the spirit of ___ , and in the name of Jesus I renounce the spirit of ___ "* (for example, anxiety, pride, anger, selfishness, rejection, guilt...).

If you have been involved in the occult: *"Jesus, I ask that you bind the spirit of ___ that came to me when I ___* (for example, went to a fortune teller, played with a Ouija board...). *And in the name of Jesus, I renounce the spirit of ___ . In the name of Jesus, I take my life back. I will not participate in these things any longer."*

When praying with others: *"Will you ask Jesus to bind the spirit of ___ and then renounce, in Jesus's name, the spirit of ___ ?* (for

example anxiety, pride, anger, selfishness, rejection, guilt…).
If the person has mentioned occult activity, *"Will you ask Jesus to bind the spirit of ___ and then renounce, in Jesus's name, any spirit that may have come to you when you ___?"*

Step 4: Take Authority

As we stated in section 3.2 of this session:

Christ's saving work on the cross merited for us the grace for our sins to be forgiven. Because of Christ's death on the cross, the gates of heaven were once again opened for us. And also, by his death and resurrection, Christ broke the power of the evil one and took back authority over this world.

Christians believe that "the world has been established and kept in being by the Creator's love; has fallen into slavery to sin but has been set free by Christ, crucified and risen to break the power of the evil one…"[85]

After renouncing the enemy, it's important to call upon Christ's authority to break the power of the evil one.

When praying for oneself: *"In the name of Jesus, I break the power of the spirit of ___. Jesus, I ask that you command it to depart right now. Thank you, Lord."*

---

85   CCC 421, quoting Vatican II, *Gaudium et Spes*, 2 §2.

When praying with others: *"Now, can you pray in the name of Jesus that the power of the spirit of ___ be broken and ask Jesus to command it to depart right now?"*[86]

Step 5: Ask for the Father's Blessing

God's good work does not stop with the removal of the curse but rather with an additional work: the restoration of his blessing. In the Book of Joel, the Lord declared, "Return to me with your whole heart" (Joel 2:12), and the people responded by fasting and praying for God's mercy. God took pity on them and declared,

> *I will repay you double*
> *what the swarming locust has eaten,*
> *The hopper, the consuming locust, and the cutter,*
> *my great army I sent against you.*
> *You will eat until you are fully satisfied,*
> *then you will praise the name of the LORD, your God,*
> *Who acts so wondrously on your behalf!*
> *My people will never again be put to shame. (Joel 2:25–26)*

When the hearts of the people turned back to God, the Lord did not just remove the swarming locusts, but he also restored the years that had been taken away because of the curse that was upon them. After breaking the authority of the enemy, we, like the Israelites, should pray to receive the blessing of God the Father.

---

86   Note the continued use of the deprecative formula. One is breaking the power of the spirit but still not addressing the spirit directly

When praying for oneself: *"Father, bless me. Let me experience your deep love for me. I am your beloved son (daughter). Fill me with your presence, with your peace, and with your joy. Amen."*

When praying with others: *"Father, bless ___. Let him (her) experience your deep love. He (She) is your beloved son (daughter). Fill him (her) with your presence, with your peace, and with your joy. Amen."*

◖ Reflect. Receive. Respond.

- Have you ever witnessed or participated in deliverance prayer? In what ways was it similar to what you've just learned? In what ways was it different?
- Pray the deliverance prayer for yourself. Reflect on your interior experience. What fruits do you see?
- How would you pray deliverance prayer with someone who is an unbeliever?

3.6

A NOTE ON
DISCERNMENT OF SPIRITS

But Peter said, "Ananias, why has Satan filled your heart so that you lied to the holy Spirit and retained part of the price of the land?" (Acts 5:3)

Oftentimes during prayer for deliverance, an individual may see the gift of discernment of spirits manifesting.

> **Discernment of Spirits:** [A]n illumination by God which enables the person to see through the outward appearance of an action or inspiration in order to judge its source. Inspirations or actions can come from three sources (or "spirits")—from God, from the person or from the devil. Having correctly discerned the source, the person can then proceed in the situation with more wisdom.[87]

---

87   Walsh, p. 100.

In keeping with the infinite creativity of the Holy Spirit, the gift
of discernment of spirits can manifest in many different ways: St.
Padre Pio was known to converse with others' guardian angels; St.
Anne Catherine Emmerich had the ability to discern if an object
had been blessed or not; St. Benedict recognized the devil when
he came disguised as a woman; and in her diary, St. Gemma writes
about being visited at night by a tiny, hairy demon.

Because lay persons are forbidden to dialogue with evil spirits, one way the gift of discernment of spirits can be very helpful
is when it manifests as the Holy Spirit revealing a sin or evil spirit
that needs to be renounced or by revealing that an individual is
in need of deliverance prayer. In this way, prayer teams are able to
help the individual pray for deliverance without taking the grave
and disobedient risk of conversing with evil.

Msgr. Walsh offers "signs" that may help one discern if an
inspiration or manifestation is **not** from God:

1.   Peace of soul is lost without any objective reason.
2.   Anxiety sets in over not following God's promptings.
3.   Sadness begins and the source cannot be detected.
4.   The person is tempted to turn back from the spiritual life and
     to abandon this life in the Spirit because it is too difficult.
5.   Fears, unknown before this, arise. Perhaps scrupulosity or pre-
     occupation with always doing the right thing is manifested.[88]

---

88   Walsh, p. 105.

It is important to remember that "discernment is the safeguard to peace of soul."[89] Scripture is very clear: "Seek peace and follow after it" (1 Peter 3:11).

Msgr. Walsh tells us, "Peace results from a union of the person's will with God's will.... Only in an atmosphere of peace does the soul grow in God's life. Even in the midst of trials permitted by God, a deep inner peace should still remain."[90] When discerning a gift of discernment of spirits, pay special attention to the presence (or lack of) peace.

---

89   Walsh, p. 106.
90   Walsh, p. 106.

3.7

GENERAL GUIDELINES FOR DELIVERANCE PRAYER

For Arise prayer teams, the following guidelines serve as a standard to help facilitate positive prayer experiences as well as protect and guard the safety of the souls involved in the prayer:

1. *The Blessed Virgin Mary:* Members of Arise prayer teams are encouraged to ask for the intercession of the Blessed Mother and to take up special devotions to her.

   > *We cannot omit a reflection about the Virgin Mary. If the firstborn creature is the Word become flesh, she who would be the means of the Incarnation must also have been present in the divine thought before every other creature. From this stems Mary's unique relationship with the Holy Trinity.*[91]

---

91   Amorth, p. 20.

St. John Vianney once said, "If you invoke the Blessed Virgin when you are tempted, she will come at once to your help, and Satan will leave you."[92]

2. ***The Laying on of Hands:*** When general prayer ministry transforms into deliverance prayer, it is not fitting for persons other than the leader to lay hands on the one receiving ministry, though hands may be extended toward that person by other team members.[93]

3. ***Speak out Loud:*** There is power in the spoken word. Demons cannot read your thoughts. When praying deliverance prayers, Arise prayer teams are encouraged to pray them out loud.

4. ***Sacramentals:*** All priests in good standing have the ability to use the Extraordinary Form Rites of Blessing over holy water, salt, and oil. These sacramentals may be given to the faithful for their own private use; however, the use of blessed oil as a sacramental is prohibited in the context of healing prayer. Blessed water and salt are permitted.

5. ***Judgement:*** Though a person confesses a grave sin, we do not have the authority to declare whether or not the individual is in a state of grace. "[A]lthough we can judge that an act is in itself a grave offense, we must entrust judgment of persons to the justice and mercy of God."[94]

---

92   St. John Vianney, as quoted at Xavier.edu.
93   Amorth, pp. 96–97.
94   CCC 1861.

6. *Use of Blessed Oil:* While a lay catechist may perform a minor exorcism as part of the Rite of Christian Initiation of Adults, the use of blessed oil in this rite is reserved to deacons and priests.[95]

7. *Major Exorcisms:* A lay person cannot perform a legitimate exorcism on a possessed person. This privilege is reserved to a priest of piety, knowledge, prudence and integrity of life, who has also obtained permission from his local ordinary to perform the exorcism.[96] Even if a lay individual obtains a copy of the Rite of Exorcism, he is forbidden to use the text to pray for the exorcism of another.[97]

8. *Exorcisms and Healing Services:* It is forbidden for the ministry of exorcism to be performed in any kind of healing service, with Mass, with the Divine Office, or within the celebration of any sacrament.[98]

9. *Public Manifestations:* As a rule, lay persons should never pray imperative deliverance prayer over someone else or attempt a major exorcism. Within a public gathering, when "it may be necessary for the leaders to take authority over any manifestation of the evil spirit to **restore the peace of the meeting**, … lay ministers should not pray binding prayers or attempt to cast out the demons—rather, they should keep speaking to the human

---

95 Leyshon, Exorcism and Prayers for Deliverance, p. 10.

96 See *CCC* 1673; Canon Law 1172§1, §2.

97 Congregation of the Doctrine of the Faith, Letter to Ordinaries Regarding Norms on Exorcism, no. 2, September 29, 1985, vatican.va.

98 Congregation for the Doctrine of the Faith, *Instruction on Prayers for Healing*, art. 8 €3.

soul being ministered to, asserting the love of Jesus, encouraging that soul to 'take control of your body and mind in the name of Jesus. Open your eyes.'"[99]

10. ***Talking to Evil Spirits:*** Only authorized exorcists may directly ask evil spirits to reveal their identities or answer other questions. Lay persons are not permitted, under any circumstance, to converse with an evil spirit. "[T]hose who are without due faculty may not conduct meetings during which invocations, to obtain release, are uttered in which demons are questioned directly and their identity sought to be known."[100] Naturally, the gift of discernment of spirits or a word of knowledge, in which the Holy Spirit reveals the name of the demon, is not the same as "conversing with an evil spirit"; because the individual has conversed with God.

11. ***Psychological Illness:*** Though sometimes overlapping, it is important to make clear a distinction between demonization and mental illness.

> *… Illness, especially psychological illness, is … the concern of medical science. Therefore, before an exorcism is performed, it is important to ascertain that one is dealing with the presence of the Evil One, and not an illness.*[101]

---

99   Leyshon, p. 18.
100 Congregation of the Doctrine of the Faith, Letter to Ordinaries Regarding Norms on Exorcism, no. 3.
101 *CCC* 1673.

12. ***Imperative vs. Deprecative:*** Considering the Church's caution regarding deliverance prayer and its preference for deprecative prayer, in deliverance prayer ministry with Arise, only deprecative prayer should be used. Prayer teams may, with great prudence, suggest spirits for the individual receiving deliverance prayer to renounce. Individuals may pray imperative prayer only over themselves.

13. ***Broadcasting:*** Deliverance ministry is not to be broadcast (on television, as a podcast, or in any other way) without specific permission from the bishop.[102]

14. ***Demons are not Created Equal:*** Like angels, demonic spirits belong to a hierarchy and have different powers, names, and manifestations. Thus it would be foolish to make an assertion, such as, "This is how evil spirits operate," or, "This is how evil spirits always manifest."[103]

◆ Reflect. Receive. Respond.

- How would you recommend deliverance prayer to a friend?
- How would you recommend deliverance prayer to a non-believer?
- How would you respond if evil spirits began manifesting while you were praying for an individual?

---

102 Congregation of the Doctrine of the Faithful, *Instruction on Prayers for Healing*, pt. II, art. 6.

103 See Cardinal Leo Joseph Suenens, *Malines Documents IV: Renewal and the Powers of Darkness.* (London: Darton, Longman & Todd, 1983), p. 155.

practicum

FOR SESSION 3

exercise 1

A PERSONAL EXERCISE OF DELIVERANCE

Directions:

Find a private place to pray through the five steps on your own. At each step, feel free to make note of anything that comes to your mind. There is power in the spoken word, so be courageous and pray out loud. Take special note of the sins of which you have repented, and confess them the next time you go to the sacrament of penance and reconciliation.

Do not pray this over someone else, but rather, invite them to pray this over themselves.

Step 1: Repent

Pray, *"Come, Holy Spirit, come. Lord, reveal to me the areas in my life where I need to ask for forgiveness and repent of my sins."* Refer to an examination of conscience if necessary.

"In the name of Jesus, I repent of ___."

Notes:

_____

_____

_____

_____

_____

Step 2: Forgive

Pray, *"Come, Holy Spirit, come. Lord, reveal to me the people in my life whom I must forgive, and grant me the graces to forgive them."*

"In the name of Jesus, I forgive ____ for ____."
Or *"Jesus, grant me the graces to desire to forgive ____ for ____."*

Notes:

_____

_____

_____

_____

_____

_____

Step 3: Renounce

Pray, *"Come, Holy Spirit, come. Reveal to me those spirits that I need to renounce."*

"Jesus, I ask that you bind the spirit of ____, and in the name of Jesus, I renounce the spirit of ____" (for example, anxiety, pride, anger, self-ishness, rejection, guilt).

If you have been involved with the occult: *"Jesus, I ask that you bind the spirit of ____ that came to me when I ____* (for example, went to a fortune teller, played with a Ouija board…). *And in the name of Jesus, I renounce the spirit of ____."*

"In the name of Jesus, I take my life back. I will have no part of these things any longer."

Notes:

_____

_____

_____

_____

_____

Step 4: Take Authority

Pray, *"Jesus, you have dominion over all creatures. Fill me with courage to believe in your authority and to break the chains of sin and oppression in my life."*

"In the name of Jesus, I break the power of the spirit of _____. Jesus, I ask you to command it to depart right now. Thank you, Lord."

Notes:

_____

_____

_____

_____

_____

Step 5: Ask for the Father's Blessing

"Father, please bless me. Let me experience your deep love for me. I am your beloved son (daughter). Fill me with your presence, with your peace, and with your joy. Amen."

Notes:

_____

_____

_____

_____

_____

exercise 2

GROUP PRAYER FOR DELIVERANCE

Directions:

Break into small groups for face-to-face intercessory prayer. Following the guidelines you have learned, offer to pray for one member of the group.

It is up to the individual to "deliver" himself or herself through repentance, forgiveness, renouncing evil, taking authority, and asking for the Father's blessing. Your goal is to guide the person through these five steps.

With any form of deliverance prayer, prayer teams should use extra gentleness and care. Remember to maintain a spirit of peace and calm during the prayer session.

THE FIVE STEPS
Repent
Forgive
Renounce
Take Authority
Ask for the Father's Blessing

Notes:

_____

_____

_____

_____

_____

_____

_____

_____

_____

_____

_____

_____

_____

_____

_____

_____

_____

_____

session 4

THE WORD GIFTS

TONGUES, INTERPRETATION, & PROPHECY

4.1

THE GIFTS ALIVE TODAY

"***True Prophecy:*** I was leading a Life in the Spirit retreat for women
from various parishes in Nebraska. On Saturday night, the plan was to
pray for the women, and I asked them to pray about what they wanted
from God. We were paired up to pray, and the first person my prayer
partner and I went to pray with was, we could tell, very apprehensive,
yet she had chosen the first seat. The strangest thing happened.

As we began to pray in tongues, I had a sensation of what it
would be like to birth a child. I felt the spiritual and physical joys of
giving birth, and I am a single woman who has never experienced that.
I whispered to my prayer partner that I had received a word but wasn't
sure if I should share it or not. My prayer partner said that she didn't
have a sense of what God was saying and for me to just speak what I felt.

I whispered into the woman's ear that I wasn't sure what this
meant, but I felt the joy of giving birth. The woman burst into tears
and seemed somewhat consoled, but she didn't explain to us what
God was doing.

At the end of the retreat, we asked the participants to share with the large group their personal experiences while on retreat. This woman was one of the first to get up. She shared that she had recently had a miscarriage, and it devastated her family. She felt that God was with her and was answering her prayer. She truly took that word as the voice of God.

The next year, I went back to Nebraska. I met Noah, the woman's new infant son, who she knew was a gift from God.

Non-Prophecy: One of the first times I prayed on a prayer team, the pastor of the parish came to me for prayer. I couldn't think or really pray because I was so nervous. I think the others in my group felt similar.

I just kind of pulled up a Scripture verse. I told him that God wanted him to read Psalm 119. As I finished speaking, I realized, to my dismay, that this is the longest psalm in the book. I really didn't know what I was saying. It was awkward. We finished our prayer of blessing, and the priest graciously said thank you and never mentioned it."

– Caroline Schutz, Dallas, TX

4.2

THE GIFTS OF TONGUES & INTERPRETATION

And they were all filled with the holy Spirit and began to speak in different tongues, as the Spirit enabled them to proclaim. (Acts 2:4)

Often called **glossolalia**, from the Greek words *glossa* (meaning "tongue" or "language") and *laleō* (meaning "to speak, talk, or make a sound"), the gift of tongues and its companion gift, interpretation, are two of the nine ministries that St. Paul lists as ordinary ministries of a healthy church community (see 1 Corinthians 12:10). Of all of the charisms of the Holy Spirit, St. Paul provides the most teaching on the gift of tongues.

"Life in the Holy Spirit fulfills the vocation of man." —CCC 1699

The Gift of Tongues: "[A] gift whereby the person prays to God in a language which he does not know, by simply "yielding" to the action of the Holy Spirit. When "praying in tongues," the person does not use his rational powers of memory or intellect which are usually employed in speaking or praying. He does use the other faculties associated with speech—the lips, the tongue, and the larynx."[104]

After Christ's ascension into heaven, the apostles gathered in the Upper Room to pray and fast as they waited on the promise of the Father (see Luke 24:49; Acts 1:4–5, 8; 2:1–4). On the Feast of Pentecost, the Holy Spirit came upon the apostles, and two distinct manifestations of the Holy Spirit involving tongues occurred. Therefore the gift of tongues can be seen as two different experiences and one companion experience:

1.   Personal Prayer Tongues[105]
2.   Public Tongues
3.   Interpretation of Tongues

Personal Prayer Tongues

In the first manifestation of the Holy Spirit on the Feast of Pentecost, the apostles in the Upper Room "were all filled with the Holy Spirit, and began to speak in different tongues as the Spirit enabled them" (Acts 2:4). In this private experience, shared only by the apostles who were gathered together, "the gift of tongues was not used to

---

104   Walsh, p. 33.

105   The gift of personal prayer tongues is commonly referred to as "prayer language" among many American charismatic groups.

teach, but to praise God, since no one was present to hear."[106] This is the first instance in Scripture of a personal prayer tongue.

> **Personal Prayer Tongue:** One of two manifestations of the charismatic gift of tongues. This permanent gift can be willed by the individual at any time and is considered a doorway to receiving other gifts of the Holy Spirit. While often appearing similar to the public gift of tongues, personal prayer tongues is meant for the individual, not for the public assembly.

Typically, the gift of a personal prayer tongue appears very early in a person's prayer life, and unlike other gifts of the Holy Spirit, it appears to be available to all. According to Msgr. Walsh, the gift "seems to be quasi-universal, so that, in general, it can be said that all should be encouraged to yield to prayer tongues."[107] St. Paul writes in his letter to the Corinthians, "I should like all of you to speak in tongues" (1 Corinthians 14:5). While considered "the doorway to the other gifts"[108] yielding to this gift is not required for salvation, nor is it the fullest or highest experience of the Holy Spirit (see 1 Corinthians 12:30).

This special gift of the Holy Spirit appears to have the following defining elements:

A Permanent Gift
Unlike the other charismatic gifts, which may not manifest with consistency (in prayers for healing, for example, sometimes a

---

106 Walsh, p. 35.

107 Walsh, p. 34.

108 Walsh, p 34.

miraculous healing occurs, and others times it does not), the gift of personal prayer tongues can be consistently yielded to at any time.[109]

In fact, "praying in tongues is a permanent ability given to a person … whereby the person, at any time, can pray to God in a language which he does not know and which is not the result of his intellectual powers."[110]

Acoustic Experience of Language

When an individual first yields to the gift, it "usually sounds like five or six words repeated in various ways."[111] As time passes and the individual continues to use the gift, it may begin to evolve. Evolution of the gift includes an increase in the number of sounds or words, change in the language, and a deeper sensitivity to the prompting (or desire) to pray in tongues.

This gift of personal prayer tongues is not gibberish; it has "all the qualities usually associated with a language—accents, patterns, cadence, etc."[112] Typically listening to prayer tongues is similar to listening to a person speak a foreign language. Nevertheless, it is important to note, "It is not necessary for prayer tongues to actually be a language. It is enough for it to be a new

---

109   Sometimes, with those who have just begun praying in personal prayer tongues, feelings of fear, insecurity, or doubt may interfere with the use of the gift. During these times, a person may feel as if he or she has lost the ability to yield to the gift of personal prayer tongues. The individual who is struggling is encouraged to seek out others to pray with.

110   Walsh, p. 40. It is important to note that, while the individual may will to yield to the gift of personal prayer tongues, he or she does not possess this gift. Like the other charismatic gifts, the power always comes from God.

111   Walsh, p. 34.

112   Walsh, p. 36.

way of praying to God, bestowed by the Spirit of God, and to be identified with the praying in tongues as described in Scripture."[113]

Translation Not Necessary

While the gift of tongues is always under the control of the individual (he may start or stop according to his will), the individual is not in control of what words he will speak, and oftentimes may not even understand what he is saying. As St. Paul says, "If I pray in a tongue, my spirit is at prayer but my mind is unproductive" (1 Corinthians 14:14).

One of the elements that differentiate private tongues and public tongues is the element of interpretation. "For one who speaks in a tongue does not speak to human beings but to God, for no one listens; he utters mysteries in spirit" (1 Corinthians 14:2). The public tongue must always have a translation; however, a personal tongue, while encouraged does not need a translation.

However, there are reported instances in which a personal prayer tongue has been interpreted. Msgr. Walsh describes a few experiences in a prayer group he led in Philadelphia:

> "A Mother Provincial from Ireland, visiting Philadelphia, was skeptical of the Charismatic Movement until she heard an Italian boy praying in Gaelic.... Two different people in the prayer community prayed in Latin and have had the prayer translated by a priest." [114]

---

113   Walsh, p. 36.
114   Walsh, p. 37.

It May Seem to Defy Reason

Speaking in a language one does not understand may seem like an offense against reason. However:

> "The gift does not offend reason although, like all of God's mysterious actions, it does ask reason to submit itself to a mystery it cannot adequately grasp.
>
> It should also be noted that speech is a very unique faculty— whereby sense organs common to the animal (tongue, lips, etc.) are used for rational activity, e.g., the communication of ideas. It seems fitting that God should "touch" this unique faculty where mind and matter converge and bestow a powerful sign of His presence."[115]

Can Pose Difficulties in Community

As praying in a personal prayer tongue is a common experience, it can happen that many members of the community would desire to gather together for a prayer meeting and all pray in their own personal prayer tongues. Participants in such experiences report feeling emotions of peace and a deep sense of the presence of the Holy Spirit.

However, pastorally, when there are strangers or newcomers to the group, the witness of a congregation praying together, each in his or her personal prayer tongue, can cause confusion, discomfort, and sometimes a rejection of the spiritual gifts. St. Paul warns of this: "[I]f the whole

---

115   Walsh, p. 36.

church meets in one place and everyone speaks in tongues, and then uninstructed people or unbelievers should come in, will they not say that you are out of your minds?" (1 Corinthians 14:23).

Imagine being in a room where people are talking to each other in a foreign language, and no one has thought to include you by translating what is being said. With this in mind, those who pray in a personal prayer tongue are encouraged to exercise charity when yielding to this gift, so as not to incite unnecessary resistance and confusion among unbelievers or inquirers. "If I speak in human and angelic tongues, but do not have love, I am a resounding gong or a clashing cymbal" (1 Corinthians 13:1).

Yielding to the Gift

The first appearance of the gift of tongues can happen in various ways. The Scriptures reveal how believers first yielded to the gift of tongues:

- The apostles yielded to the gift after a period of praying and fasting in the Upper Room. All of the sudden, they were overcome with the Holy Spirit "and began to speak in different tongues, as the Spirit enabled them to proclaim" (Acts 2:4).
- Those at Ephesus first yielded when Paul laid his hands upon them after baptism: "And when Paul laid [his] hands upon them, the holy Spirit came upon them, and they spoke in tongues and prophesied" (Acts 19:6).
- The Gentiles of Caesarea first yielded to the gift of tongues after hearing Peter preach the Gospel of Jesus Christ:

*While Peter was still speaking these things, the holy Spirit fell
upon all who were listening to the word. The circumcised believers who had accompanied Peter were astounded that the gift of
the holy Spirit should have been poured out on the Gentiles also,
for they could hear them speaking in tongues and glorifying God.
(Acts 10:44–46)*

For baptized Christians who desire to pray in tongues, it is encouraged that the individual ask God for the gift, and to live in such a
manner that helps dispose the individual to receiving this indwelling
of the Holy Spirit. Here are some additional notes on welcoming the
gift of tongues:

- The first time a person yields to tongues, he or she may experience certain consolations (such as a rush of energy, warmth,
a strong and overwhelming sense of peace); however, this experience of consolation is not necessary to ensure the authen-
ticity of the gift. For many persons, praying in their prayer
tongues can come as naturally and unemotionally as speaking.
- For various reasons (poor timing, nervousness, insecurities,
poor environment, doubt, God's will, and so on), the person
may not be able to yield to the gift of tongues. The practicum
may need to be repeated with this individual.
- From Msgr. Walsh:

  *It sometimes happens that a person who has "yielded to tongues"
  will come up the next day and say that he has "lost the gift." It is
  much like the little child who rides a bike and later says he "forgot
  how to do it."*

If this happens, the person should be helped again to yield. He [or she] should also be encouraged to pray frequently in tongues so [as to gain] confidence in using the gift.[116]

Exercise 1 in the practicum portion of this session is specifically intended to help an individual yield to the gift of tongues.

Benefits of Personal Prayer Tongues

There are many benefits to praying in tongues.

Even with years of experience, charismatic Catholics have not uncovered all of the effects of this gift. However, the following can be listed:

- It helps the individual fulfill Christ's command to pray always.
- It is an aid to recollection and leads to more fervent prayer.
- It is the doorway to charismatic ministries—the use of prayer tongues somehow sensitizes the person to yield to other charismatic activity of the Holy Spirit.
- It is a personal, concrete sign of God's action within.
- It is a powerful weapon against Satan.
- It is an effective means of intercessory prayer, especially when the person does not know exactly for what to pray.[117]

---

116   Walsh, p. 39.
117   Walsh, pp. 37–38.

Summary on the Gift of Personal Prayer Tongues

∗ Typically appears very early in a prayer life; however, it can appear at any time, as its appearance is dependent on the movement of God, not the merit of the individual

∗ Is meant primarily for the individual

∗ Is quasi-universal, so all persons can be encouraged to yield to prayer tongues

∗ Is a permanent ability

∗ Is freely willed

∗ Does not require translation

∗ Can act as a doorway to receiving the other gifts of the Holy Spirit

Public Tongues

The second manifestation of the Holy Spirit also occurs on the Feast of Pentecost, when the apostles walk outside and begin preaching to a large crowd: "Now there were devout Jews from every nation under heaven staying in Jerusalem. At this sound, they gathered in a large crowd, but they were confused because each one heard them speaking in his own language" (Acts 2:5–6). Here the gift of tongues was a supernatural way for the Holy Spirit to communicate with the crowd that had gathered. The gift was meant for public use, and it was understood by the members of the assembly.

> **Public Prayer Tongues:** "A passing manifestation of the Holy Spirit to an individual … during a charismatic prayer meeting, whereby the person is prompted to speak aloud in tongues, which must be followed by use of the companion

gift of interpretation. This use of the gifts of tongues and interpretation is very akin to the gift of prophecy."[118]

Here are some defining elements of public tongues:

A Passing Manifestation

Unlike a personal prayer tongue, the gift of public tongues is not a permanent gift but rather (like other charismatic gifts) a passing manifestation of God's power. Typically, an individual is prompted by the Holy Spirit to address the community in tongues.

> Usually, the person is a mature member of the community who has become sensitive to God's movements. The sensitivity takes into account the circumstances of the prayer meeting and an internal touch or anointing. As the person recognizes God's movement, he yields to it by an act of the will, speaking aloud, by himself, in tongues. [119]

To Be Interpreted

How the public tongues differs from personal prayer tongues is that there should always be an interpretation. St. Paul stresses this multiple times to the church in Corinth:

> Now, brothers, if I should come to you speaking in tongues, what good will I do you if I do not speak to you by way of

118 Walsh, p. 51.
119 Walsh, p. 54.

*revelation, or knowledge, or prophecy, or instruction?...
[I]f you, because of speaking in tongues, do not utter intel-
ligible speech, how will anyone know what is being said?
For you will be talking to the air. (1 Corinthians 14:6, 9)*

*I give thanks to God that I speak in tongues more than any
of you, but in the church I would rather speak five words
with my mind, so as to instruct others also, than ten thou-
sand words in a tongue. (1 Corinthians 14:18–19)*

St. Paul also encourages an interpretation so that the community
can be edified:

*[I]f you pronounce a blessing [with] the spirit, how shall
the one who holds the place of the uninstructed say the
"Amen" to your thanksgiving, since he does not know what
you are saying? For you may be giving thanks very well,
but the other is not built up. (1 Corinthians 14:16–17)*

A Sense of Order

Our God is a God of order, and the use of public prayer tongues
must be done in a way that respects this nature of God. St. Paul
instructs, "So, [my] brothers, strive eagerly to prophesy, and do
not forbid speaking in tongues, but everything must be done
properly and in order" (1 Corinthians 14:39–40). He recommends, "If anyone speaks in a tongue, let it be two or at most
three, and each in turn, and one should interpret. But if there is
no interpreter, the person should keep silent in the church and
speak to himself and to God" (1 Corinthians 14:27–28).

Here St. Paul makes two recommendations:

1. Those addressing the community through the gift of tongues may speak one at a time (not together or talking over each other) with an interpretation to follow.

2. If there is no interpreter, tongues must be prayed privately and quietly.

Summary on the Gift of Public Tongues

* Is a passing manifestation, prompted by the Holy Spirit
* Must be followed by the companion gift of interpretation
* Should be done in an orderly way, with no more than two or three persons speaking, one at a time

Interpretation of Tongues

Since the gift of public prayer tongues requires an interpretation, it is important to define this companion gift:

> **Interpretation:** "The gift of interpretation is the power given to an individual to speak, in the vernacular, the general meaning of whatever was said aloud in the gift of tongues."[120]

When interpreted, the gift of public tongues helps to build up the Church. St. Paul identifies four things that make the use of public tongues profitable: "revelation, knowledge, prophecy," and "word of instruction" (1 Corinthians 14: 6).

---

120 Walsh, p. 53.

Yielding to Interpretation

In keeping with the creativity of the Holy Spirit and the individuality of the person, the gift of interpretation can take many forms. An individual may hear another person praying in tongues as if that person were "speaking in his own language" (Acts 2:6). Others may experience words or phrases coming to mind after hearing the tongues. St. Paul encourages those who speak in tongues to pray for the gift of interpretation (see 1 Corinthians 14:13).

To yield to this gift of interpretation, it is first recommended that one ask God in faith for the gift of understanding. "[T]he person should make an act of childlike faith, that God will speak to him."[121] It is important that the individual not try to make up appropriate words or invent an interpretation but rather wait for the inspiration. "Often, as the words come together in a sentence, the person will be 'urged' to speak it forth for the good of the community."[122] The community may then test the interpretation to discern if the word truly was from the Holy Spirit.

After much time yielding to the gift of interpretation, this gift of the Holy Spirit has the potential to develop in the person as a ministry of interpretation. In this manner we can be like St. Paul, who said, "So what is to be done? I will pray with the spirit, but I will also pray with the mind. I will sing praise with the spirit, but I will also sing praise with the mind" (1 Corinthians 14:15).

Testing the Gift

Like the other gifts of the Spirit, interpretation must be tested. St. John

---

121   Walsh, p. 55.
122   Walsh, p. 55.

advises: "Beloved, do not trust every spirit but test the spirits to see whether they belong to God, because many false prophets have gone out into the world" (1 John 4:1).

Msgr. Walsh counsels: ... *[A]fter the use of the gift of tongues,... a certain stillness or quiet sets in (and should be deliberately fostered). During this period, the people ask God to speak to them. Frequently, members experience the charismatic activity of phrases or sentences coming to mind. These thoughts must be tested to see if they really are from God. If the person feels they are, then the words should be spoken aloud.*[123]

The following are indications that an interpretation is true:
- Multiple members of the group receive the same interpretation.
- The interpretation brings forth the good fruits of the Holy Spirit, such as joy and peace among the members gathered.

"If neither of these ... two is present, then the group might suspend judgment on whether or not God has truly spoken."[124]

Growing in the Gift of Interpretation
An individual can promote growth in the gift of interpretation in various ways. While not an exhaustive list, the following are some recommendations:
1. Ask God for the gift of interpretation.
2. Experiment with the gift while in prayer with a private prayer group or class members. Msgr. Walsh teaches: ... *[I]f while a person is speaking in tongues, the Spirit seems to prompt the*

---

123 Walsh, p. 55.
124 Walsh, p. 55.

individual with a thought, the person, after a short period of prayerful discernment, should speak those words for the community, later accepting the community's discernment on the gift [of interpretation].[125]

3. Pray for the grace to overcome any self-consciousness or fear regarding addressing the group with an interpretation.

4. Pray for the wisdom to be sensitive to the prompting of the Holy Spirit. "[T]he person should not wait for perfect certitude that his words are from the Spirit. A stepping out in faith is always an important element in growing in the gift."[126]

Summary on the Gift of Interpretation of Tongues

∗ Always follows the gift of public tongues
∗ Is a companion gift to public tongues
∗ Is profitable for the community when it brings either revelation, knowledge, prophecy, or a word of instruction
∗ Does not need to be an exact translation but rather a "sense" of what God is saying

Abuses of the Gifts of Tongues and Interpretation

The following examples are potential abuses of the gift of tongues and interpretation:

Counterfeit Tongues

Just as a person can yield to the Holy Spirit and pray in tongues,

---

125   Walsh, p. 56.
126   Walsh, p. 56.

an individual can also, in very rare circumstances, yield to a false spirit. One can recognize counterfeit tongues because typically, such tongues "are uncontrolled, harsh, and disturbing. Discernment of false tongues is fairly easy for any experienced leader."[127]

If an individual knows that he or she has prayed in this counterfeit way, the person should be encouraged to speak with a priest regarding what may have opened the individual to this activity. "Usually, it is rooted in the kingdom of darkness."[128]

Public Use without Prompting

Sometimes, whether out of ignorance, immaturity, inexperience, or a need for acceptance and approval, an individual may publicly address the assembly in their personal prayer tongue without having been prompted by the Holy Spirit to do so. In these cases, there may be no appearance of the companion gift of interpretation, and the congregation is not edified because there is a lack of understanding.

False Interpretation

"The gift of interpretation is open to misuse, since the charismatic community is usually aware of St. Paul's teaching that interpretation should follow the gift of tongues. A certain pressure can be present to 'force' an interpretation at this time. Obviously, the wrong use of the gift of tongues can easily lead to a similar wrong use of the companion gift of interpretation."[129]

---

127 Walsh, p. 57.
128 Walsh, p. 57.
129 Walsh, p. 57.

◆ Reflect. Receive. Respond.

- Have you ever witnessed anyone pray in tongues? What was your experience?
- In what ways do you think the gifts of tongues and interpretation can help an individual? A community?

4.3

THE GIFT OF PROPHECY

Strive eagerly for the spiritual gifts, above all that you may prophesy.
(1 Corinthians 14:1)

St. Paul lists the gift of prophecy as one of the nine regular charismatic ministries that should be present in every local church.

Prophecy comes from the Greek word *prophetia*, which means "gift of interpreting the will of God." In Hebrew, the word for *prophet* is *nabî*, which means "interpreter and mouthpiece of God."

> "Finally, charisms are not personal achievements but are sovereign manifestations of the Holy Spirit."
> – Secretariat for Promoting Christian Unity, 1976

The first person to receive the title of prophet (*nabî*) in the Old Testament was Abraham. (see Genesis 20:7). Many prophets emerged after Abraham, including Aaron, Isaiah, Jeremiah, and others. God made his will known to these prophets in various ways: To some, he would appear in a vision; to others, God would reveal his thoughts in a dream; and with some, he would speak face-to-face (see Numbers 12:6–8).

While Jesus never explicitly called himself a prophet, he revealed himself as one when he said, "No prophet is without honor except in his native place" (see Matthew 13:57), and again when he permitted others to call him a prophet (see Luke 7:16). "Jesus fulfilled the messianic hope of Israel in his threefold office of priest, prophet, and king."[130]

Christ demonstrated prophecy multiple times in the Gospels, including prophesying Peter's denial; the passion, death, and resurrection; and the many wonders the apostles would be able to work in his name (see Matthew 26:30-35; John 14:12). This special gift of prophecy was one of the many gifts bestowed upon the apostles in the Upper Room, and is still alive and active in the Church today.

True Prophecy

A true prophecy "can enlighten both the individual and the community about … graces to seek from God, actions to undertake, attitudes to inculcate or to remove, [and] events to prepare for."[131] Prophecy typically brings edification, exhortation, or comfort to a person or community. The utterances can be about present or future events.

Since prophecy is communicated through a human person, there is a risk of mixing in the human spirit and even uttering false prophecies. "Since prophecy is an extremely powerful gift, it must be understood, [be] surrounded with safeguards and be subject to leadership."[132] Here we will discuss the nature and practice of prophecy as well as the safeguards that should surround it.

---

130   *CCC* 436
131   Walsh, p. 60.
132   Walsh, p. 59.

Prophecy: "It is the gift whereby God manifests to man His own thoughts so that a message may be given for the individual or for a group of individuals, or for the community."[133]

Prophecy can be given either publicly or privately, directed toward the entire community or a single individual.

Public Prophecy is shared in a public forum—for example, during a prayer service that has been advertised to the public.

Private Prophecy is shared either to a single individual or a private, closed group—for example, members of one's personal support group.

Personal Prophecy, given publicly or privately, is meant exclusively for an individual as opposed to an entire group.

The gift of prophecy shares the following elements:

A Gift for All

In the Old Testament, Moses says to Joshua, "If only all the people of the LORD were prophets! If only the LORD would bestow his spirit on them!" (Numbers 11:29). In the New Testament, St. Paul states, "Now I should like all of you to speak in tongues, but even more to prophesy" (1 Corinthians 14:5). The Scriptures are suggesting that it is desirable for *all* members of the faithful to yield to the gift of prophecy. "For

---

133 Walsh, p. 60.

you can all prophesy one by one, so that all may learn and all
be encouraged" (1 Corinthians 14:31).

Many Different Forms

A prophecy can come to an individual in many different ways: a
dream, vision, thought, and sometimes even an auditory sound
(see Numbers 12:6–8). Msgr. Walsh reflects on a common
experience of prophecy among individuals:

> … [T]he person perceives certain words or phrases going
> through his mind. Or perhaps a certain picture comes into
> the imagination seemingly "out of nowhere." In other words,
> the person perceives God's action and that divine activity
> results in an intelligible message. The ways this occurs seem
> to vary greatly. Some receive whole sentences while others
> seem only to have a word at a time. Others have no words,
> but the sense of a message. After a while, the person recog-
> nizes and understands how God touches them in prophecy.
> One aspect that seems common is that the use of prayer
> tongues sensitizes the person to yield to this gift.[134]

Initial Understanding Not Necessary

It is not necessary that the person delivering the prophecy
understand its meaning. Nevertheless, every effort should
be made by the person to deliver the message as it has been
received.

---

134   Walsh, p. 62.

*"... [The person prophesying] might not know just what it
means. The person for whom the prophecy is meant will
know what it means. Again, discernment must be used,
but if the person [giving the prophecy] ... has no idea
of the problem or decision facing the other person, then
more credence would be given to it as coming from God
than if the person ... were aware, by natural means, of
the other's problem.*[135]

Can be Unemotional

Sometimes an individual delivering or recieving a prophecy
may be given consolations, such as an intense sense of God's
presence and peace. These consolations are not essential to an
authentic gift and thus are to be received with gratitude.

Good Fruit

A true prophecy edifies, instructs, exhorts, or comforts the
individual or community receiving the prophecy. The good
fruits of the Holy Spirit follow true prophecy. "True prophecy
tends to bestow peace and joy, even when it points out the
faults of the community."[136]

Yielding to Prophecy

If an individual thinks that God may be working within him in this
way, "The person should remain deep in prayer, somewhat passive
and childlike, asking God to help him cooperate with this grace.

---

135   Walsh, p. 68.
136   *Key to the Catholic Charismatic Renewal*, Msgr. Vincent Walsh p. 53.

He should allow God to influence his intellect, memory and imagination and begin to search out what God wants him to say. As he
actively cooperates, he will become somewhat certain that God is
moving him to prophesy and will at least be certain of the beginning
words. As he speaks these [words] "in faith," the rest are given."[137]

Confirming a Prophecy

After a prophecy has been shared, it is important that the word be
discerned to determine if it is true prophecy, false prophecy, or
non-prophecy. "As a person 'steps out in faith' and delivers a prophecy, he is still not perfectly certain that his prophecy is from God.
'Confirmation' is necessary so the person and the community obtain
the needed certitude."[138]

1. **True Prophecy:** "a message from God meant for the community or for the individual."[139] This prophecy does not contradict Church teaching. It typically bears one or more of the
   following signs:
   - The person receiving the prophecy has received a
     similar prophetic message before. For example, three
     individuals might independently approach a woman
     and give the same or a similar prophetic word.
   - The prophecy comes true.
   - The words "resonate" with the individual or community
     receiving the prophecy.

---

137   Walsh, p. 63.

138   Walsh, p. 63.

139   Walsh, p. 64.

- The prophecy "corresponds to the internal word of
  what God is doing within the person—in this way
  God's internal and external activities harmonize."[140]
- The fruits of the Holy Spirit are present.

2. **Non-Prophecy:** "a general statement—usually pious or Scrip-
    tural in form, which comes from the person's human spirit
    rather than from God's Holy Spirit. It is usually harmless to the
    group and differs from true prophecy because it does not come
    from God and lacks power to build up the community or en-
    courage the members."[141] Here are some signs of non-prophecy:

    - The prophecy does not "resonate" with anyone in the
      community or, in the case of personal prophecy, with
      the individual receiving it.
    - If it regards future events, the prophecy does not
      come true.
    - The prophecy doesn't bring about edification, exhor-
      tation, or comfort, but it also doesn't bring bad fruit.
      "Non-prophecy brings forth no fruit—good or bad.
      Although not disturbing, it does not possess the power
      of the true charismatic gift."[142]

3. **False Prophecy:** "an utterance which comes from the evil spirit
    and brings with it many harmful effects, such as disruption of
    the prayer meeting or confusion among leaders or members of

---

140   Walsh, p. 72.
141   Walsh, p. 64.
142   Walsh, p. 65.

the prayer community. False prophecy is usually very rare and most prayer communities seem to have more of a problem with non-prophecy." Here are some signs of false prophecy:[143]

- The prophecy causes disruption, fear, shame, turmoil, confusion, anxiety, or other bad fruits.
- The prophecy leads the person or community to do something contrary to the will of God. For example, a prophetic word that encourages a person to violate God's law or a Church teaching.
- There is a lack of peace.

General Guidelines for Prophecy

Prophecy requires many safeguards. Please consider the following:

1. *Be discerning about the purity of a prophecy:* Even when God is speaking, the prophet's theological background and emotional state, as well as the atmosphere in which the prophecy is being delivered, can lead the individual to modify, reverse, or even add to a prophecy, thus distorting the prophetic word. "Just as water passing through a rusty pipe comes out as rusty water, so in prophecy God's message can be modified by the person's human condition, even though the person is truly moved by God's charismatic activity."[144] When hearing a prophecy, understand that "parts of a prophecy might be from God and some from the person."[145]

---

143   Walsh, p. 64.

144   Walsh, p. 66.

145   Walsh, p. 67.

2. ***Give it time:*** For predictive prophecies, "the 'time' element ... is extremely difficult to discern. A prophecy, therefore, could be true but its fulfillment still be many years away."[146]

3. ***Look for the fruit of the Spirit:*** True prophecy will bring about the fruits of the Holy Spirit, even when the prophecy is an admonition. Emotions such as anxiety, shame, fear, and so on are typically indications that the delivered message is not a true and pure prophecy.

4. ***Share prophecy honestly and openly:*** Because the purity of the prophesy is often at risk, it is important that the prophesy be communicated to the community or individual in a way that permits the other to accept or reject the prophecy. Ask, for example, "Does that resonate with you?" or, "Does that mean anything to you?"

5. ***Submit public prophecy to proper discernment:*** When receiving a prophetic word for the public, the individual is encouraged to first humbly submit the word for testing and discernment by the pastors of the Church. "The illusion that because one's prophecies or other charisms come from God they therefore need no discernment or oversight is a dangerous temptation to spiritual pride. As Scriptures make clear, every charism is subject to discernment (1 Cor 14:21; 1 Thes 5:21; 1 John 4:1). "No one owns the charism he or she has been given. No charism dispenses a person from reference and submission

---

146   Walsh, p. 67.

to the Pastors of the Church.[147] This is doubly important if the prophetic word is a rebuke or a directive prophecy.

6. ***Beware of certain prophecies:*** While permitted with good discernment in a *private forum*, during a public prayer service, Arise prayer ministry persons are strongly discouraged from sharing the following: directive prophecies, prophecies involving specific dates, and prophecies about future spousal relationships.

◈ Reflect. Receive. Respond.

- What has been your experience with the gift of prophecy?
- What is the difference between a natural word of encouragement and the supernatural gift of prophecy?
- What personal safeguards can you implement in your own life to try to preserve the purity of a prophetic word?

---

147   *Christifideles Laici,* 24

practicum

FOR SESSION 4

exercise 1

YEILDING TO TONGUES

Goal

To help an individual yield to the gift of personal prayer tongues.

While the gift of personal prayer tongues can manifest in various ways, it is possible to help a member of the community yield to the gift. This practicum aims to do just that.[148]

For this practicum, there are three people involved:

1. **Learner:** the individual who desires to yield to the gift of tongues
2. **Helper:** the individual who will pray in tongues
3. **Intercessor:** the individual who will join the prayer session solely as an intercessor and accountability partner during the practicum. The presence of the intercessor is not explicitly necessary but helpful and encouraged.

Step 1

Identify **Helper** members of the community. These should be people who are both confident in their own gift of tongues and open to helping another member of the group yield to tongues

Allow potential **Learners** to recognize who these **Helper** individuals are.

---

148   The Holy Spirit moves when and how he wills; therefore, this practicum is not to be considered a sure way to receive the gift of tongues but rather a help.

Step 2

Identify volunteers who desire to pray as **Intercessors**.

Step 3

Allow **Learners**, individuals who desire to be helped in yielding to the gift of tongues, to approach one of the identified **Helper** members. It is important that there be a spirit of trust, mutual respect, and comfort between the Helper and the Learner. Both the Helper and the Learner should have the freedom to mutually agree to enter into the practicum, and neither should be judged or shamed for avoiding the practicum out of a lack of trust, respect, or sense of comfort.

Step 4

Once **Learner** and **Helper** have been established, they should together select an **Intercessor** to join the prayer session. The Helper will be the prayer leader for this prayer session. If an Intercessor is not available, the prayer may still continue.

Step 5

Begin the prayer by calling upon the presence of the Holy Spirit and giving praise to God. The **Helper** should ask God to remove any barriers, emotional or psychological, or any sins that may block the Learner's ability to yield to the gift of tongues. The Helper should ask God to grant this grace of the Holy Spirit to the Learner. The Intercessor is to intercede for these intentions throughout the prayer session.

Step 6

The **Helper** begins to pray in his personal prayer tongue. The **Learner** should then leave aside English (or other native language), as well as the rational activity of the memory and intellect, and imitate the prayer tongue of the Helper.

> *.... By coming out with the first few strange syllables, the person yields to the gift of prayer tongues and discovers himself praising God in an entirely different language than that of the person who helped him yield to this gift....*
>
> *In bestowing this gift, God does not force a person's mouth open. The normal procedure is for the person to take the first steps in faith by moving his [or her] lips and allowing God to fill ... [his or her mouth] with prayer tongues.*[149]

The **Intercessor** is to pray quietly for both the Helper and the Learner during this time. If the Learner has difficulty yielding to tongues, the Helper may encourage the Learner to repeat a prayer, such as "Come, Holy Spirit," or simply "Jesus," as the Helper and Intercessor continue to pray.

If the Learner still does not yield to tongues, remember what we said in section 1.3: The coming of the Spirit is not under human control. Encourage the Learner to continue to petition God for the gift. It may also be good to repeat the practicum, immediately or at a later time.

---

149   Walsh, p. 39.

Step 7

End the practicum with a prayer of thanksgiving to God.

exercise 2

DEVELOPING A GIFT OF PROPHECY

Goal

To help an individual grow in trust and confidence in the prompt-ings of the Holy Spirit through journaling, discernment, and action.

Step 1: Write It All Down

Begin your day with the mindset that you will journal throughout the day, writing down any insights you believe are coming from God. For example, if while praying you sense or hear a comforting word, write it down. If while driving to work you get a sense about a person or circumstance, write it down. If you're at Mass and you see an individual and are struck with a Scripture verse to share with him or her, write this prompting down. A written log will create a sense of focus and accountability.

Step 2: Discern

When you receive a prompting, begin basic discernment. Ask yourself:

- Is this from myself or the Holy Spirit? Have I added my own thoughts, ideas, imagination? Have I added my own bias?
- Is this revelation bringing about good fruit? Does it make me feel peaceful? Or am I anxious and fearful?
- Does this revelation agree with or contradict Church teaching? (If the word contradicts Church teaching, it is not from God, and thus not true prophecy.)
- Would this prophetic word bring exhortation, comfort, and edification (see 1 Corinthians 14:3)?
- Is the present environment one that is conducive to sharing this prophecy?

Step 3: Submit Word for Testing

After you have interiorly discerned that the word is intended for another person, test it by sharing it with a trustworthy person who is gifted in prophecy. If the person agrees that the word is from the Lord and is appropriate to share, proceed to step 4.

Step 4: Action

If the word regards an action you should take (such as make a decision, write someone a letter, volunteer for an activity), then proceed with that action.

If the word concerns someone else, share it with that person. Be conscious of your phrasing. Avoid saying to someone, "The Holy Spirit said XYZ." Instead, use phrases like "I'm getting this sense of the Scripture Romans 8. Will you look at that and let me know if it means anything to you?" or, "I was just praying for you, and I felt this word come to mind, 'Be still and trust.' Does that resonate with you at all?"

Step 5: Consider the Fruit

Scripture says that we shall know a prophecy by its fruits (see Matthew 7:16). After taking action, discern the fruits. Was the prophecy right? Did it bring about the fruits of the Holy Spirit? Did any words come to pass?

If some inspirations were correct but some were not, consider how you received each inspiration. Continue to grow in your ability to yield to the Holy Spirit.

POPCORN PROPHECY

Goal

To help individuals grow in the gift of prophecy by refining their listening skills through immediate feedback.

Step 1

Divide the class into two lines, Line A (which is stationary) and Line B (which will move). Have Line A and Line B face each other. If there is an odd number of persons, have the extra person stand at the end of Line A.

Step 2

Allow the individuals who are facing each other to ask God for an encouraging word or prophecy to share with the individuals in front of them. Wait on the Spirit.

Step 3

People in Line A should speak the word to the persons in front of them. Allow the persons in Line B to give immediate feedback to the persons in Line A: "Yes, this resonates," or, "Only part of that resonates," or, "Nope, nothing." Then allow the persons in Line B to share prophetic words with Line A. Again discuss. **Be honest** when giving feedback.

Step 4

When the moderator calls "Time," Line B will shift one person to the right. The person at the end of Line B should walk to the front of the line. Repeat steps 2 and 3.

session 5

HEALING PRAYER

5.1

SUFFERING & REDEMPTION

A large number of people from the towns in the vicinity of Jerusalem also gathered, bringing the sick and those disturbed by unclean spirits, and they were all cured. (Acts 5:16)

With a bite of a piece of fruit, "evil, pain, sin and death entered into the world."[150] Old Testament writers understood that "illness is mysteriously linked to sin and evil."[151] In fact, throughout the Old Testament, sick persons beseech God for healing while confessing the just punishment for their sins (cf. Psalm 37; 40; 106:17–21). Many Israelites believed that if a person was sick or suffering, it was because the hurting individual was receiving punishment for his sins.

The apostles shared this perspective. "Rabbi," they asked, "who sinned, this man or his parents, that he was born blind?" (John 9:2).

---

150   Amorth, p. 21.

151   *CCC* 1502.

Jesus's response challenged the old idea: "Neither he nor his parents

"Illness and suffering have always been among the gravest problems confronted in human life. In illness, man experiences his powerlessness, his limitations, and his finitude. Every illness can make us glimpse death." —CCC 1500

sinned; it is so that the works of God might be made visible through him" (John 9:3). Jesus thus revealed that "while it is true that suffering has a meaning as punishment, *it is not true that all suffering is a consequence of a fault.*"[152] Going back to the Old Testament, this truth is re-

vealed at length in the Book of Job, in which a just and righteous man endures great suffering.

So it would seem that, just as God "makes his sun rise on the bad and the good, and causes rain to fall on the just and the unjust" (Matthew 5:45), suffering befalls both the sinner and the innocent. The experience of suffering is a common and shared experience; all mankind is subject to it. "Hence arises the question of a religious approach to its cure."[153]

Mankind longs for redemption and for a cure to suffering and illness. The prophet Isaiah spoke of a time when:

> *He will destroy death forever.*
> *The Lord GOD will wipe away*
> *the tears from all faces;*
> *The reproach of his people he will remove*
> *from the whole earth; for the LORD has spoken. (Isaiah 25:8)*

---

152   Pope John Paul II, *Salvifici Doloris*, Apostolic Letter on the Christian Meaning of Suffering, no. 11, February 11, 1984, www.vatican.va.

153   P.D. Letter, "Christian Healing," in *New Catholic Encyclopedia* (Washington, D.C.: McGraw-Hill, 1967), pp. 960–961.

This prophecy would be fulfilled in the person of Jesus Christ, who was not subject to illness; rather, illness was subject to him.

> ... *In the public activity of Jesus, his encounters with the sick are not isolated, but continual. He healed many through miracles, so that miraculous healings characterized his activity: "Jesus went around to all the towns and villages, teaching in their synagogues, proclaiming the Gospel of the kingdom, and curing every disease and illness" (Matthew 9:35; cf. 4:23). These healings are signs of his messianic mission (cf. Luke 7:20–23). They manifest the victory of the kingdom of God over every kind of evil, and become the symbol of the restoration to health of the whole human person, body and soul....[154]*

However, the *Catechism* notes of Christ's public ministry,

> *[H]e did not heal all the sick. His healings were signs of the coming of the Kingdom of God. They announced a more radical healing: the victory over sin and death through his Passover. On the cross Christ took upon himself the whole weight of evil and took away the "sin of the world," of which illness is only a consequence. By his passion and death on the cross Christ has given a new meaning to suffering: it can henceforth configure us to him and unite us with his redemptive Passion.[155]*

---

154 Congregation for the Doctrine of the Faith, Instruction on Prayers for Healing, pt. I, no. 1.

155 *CCC* 1505, quoting John 1:29; cf. Isaiah 54:4–6.

Christ's victory, power, and authority over the evil of suffering and illness did not end with his resurrection and ascension into heaven but rather continues in his Church.

Before his ascension into heaven, Christ called together the apostles and taught that: "These signs will accompany those who believe: They will lay hands on the sick, and they will recover" (Mark 16:17-18). With this direction, the apostles went out and began to lay hands on the sick.

Their results are well recorded in the Book of Acts. For example, Peter cured Aeneas of paralysis, and Paul healed a crippled man and raised Eutychus from the dead (see Acts 9:33–34; 14:8–10; 20:9–12). This practice of laying hands on the sick and experiencing the miracle of healing in the name of Jesus continued in the early Church as a normal ministry, a shared experience of both the laity and the clergy.[156]

The display of Christ's victory over suffering was a driving force in the growth and spread of Christianity in the first and second centuries, as attested by Church fathers:

> … [S]ome of you are becoming disciples in the name of Christ, and quitting the path of error; who are also receiving gifts, each as he is worthy, illumined through the name of this Christ. For one receives the spirit of understanding, another of counsel, another of strength, another of healing, another of foreknowledge, another of teaching, and another of the fear of God.[157]

---

156 While lay persons could pray for healing and experience Christ's miraculous indwelling, they did not administer the official sacraments of healing (penance and reconciliation and anointing of the sick), as these are reserved to the consecrated priesthood.

157 Justin Martyr († AD 165), *Dialogues with Trypho*, chap. 36, in Alexander Roberts and James Donaldson, eds., *The Writings of the Fathers down to A.D. 325*, vol. 1, An-

*... What nobler than to tread underfoot the gods of the nations—
to exorcise evil spirits—to perform cures—to seek divine reveal-
ings—to live to God?...*[158]

While in later centuries the regular activity of the Holy Spirit declined
among the laity, the charismatic gift of healing remained. This is
evident in the lives of the saints (both male and female), whose many
extraordinary deeds have been well recorded. In fact, in the canon-
ization process for saints, "authentic miracles and cures have been
required as signs from heaven confirming their heroic virtue."[159]

This gift is also evident in the Church's practice of the
sacraments of healing, anointing of the sick and penance and
reconciliation. It can be said, "Prayer for the restoration of health
is therefore part of the Church's experience in every age, including our own."[160] Yet somehow, the idea that the charismatic gift of
healing is a ministry reserved for the chosen few (to the exclusion
of others) developed in many Christian circles.

While St. Paul does indicate that the gift of healing is given
to some and not all (cf. 1 Corinthians 12:30), he never says that the
faithful should not strive for the gift, nor do the Scriptures forbid
persons to ask God for the gift of healing and to pray expectantly for
the healing of others. To the contrary, the Scriptures are filled with
instructions to petition God for healing:

te-Nicene Fathers (New York: Charles Scribner, 1905), p. 214.

158 Tertullian († AD 240), *De Spectaculis*, chap. 29, in Alexander Roberts et al, eds., Latin
Christianity, vol. 3, *The Ante-Nicene Fathers* (New York: Cosimo, 2007), p. 91.

159 Letter, P.D. (1967). Christian Healing. *In the New Catholic Encyclopedia* (pp. 960-961).
Washington, DC: McGraw-Hill.

160 Congregation for the Doctrine of the Faith, Instruction on Prayers for Healing, introduction.

My son, when you are ill, do not delay,
but pray to God, for it is he who heals. (Sirach 38:9)

[Pray] for one another, that you may be healed. The fervent
prayer of a righteous person is very powerful. (James 5:16)

And Paul tells us to "strive eagerly for the greatest spiritual gifts," certainly including the gift of healing (1 Corinthians 12:31).

Thus the Church teaches, "Not only is it praiseworthy for individual members of the faithful to ask for healing for themselves and others, but the Church herself asks the Lord for the health of the sick in her Liturgy," and, "It is licit [permitted] for every member of the faithful to pray to God for healing."[161]

◆ Reflect. Receive. Respond.

- Do you believe that God could work through you to bring healing to his people? Why or why not?
- What is holding you back from praying expectantly for the healing of the sick?
- How would your life change if you became open to a ministry of healing?

---

161   Instruction on Prayers for Healing, pt. I, no. 2; pt. II, art. 1.

5.2

HEALING DEFINED

Is anyone among you sick? He should summon the presbyters of the church, and they should pray over him and anoint [him] with oil in the name of the Lord. (James 5:14)

The call to participate in Christ's ministry as healer is universal among Christians. The Catechism tells us:

> *The Lord Jesus Christ, physician of our souls and bodies, who forgave the sins of the paralytic and restored him to bodily health [see Mark 2:1–12], has willed that his Church continue, in the power of the Holy Spirit, his work of healing and salvation.*[162]

The Church answers this call in two ways: through the **sacraments of healing** and through the **charism of healing**.

---

162 CCC 1421

The Sacraments of Healing

The two sacraments of healing are **penance and reconciliation** and **anointing of the sick**.

> **Penance and Reconciliation:** One of the seven sacraments of the Church, whereby a member of the faithful confesses personal sins to a priest, obtains divine mercy for those sins, and is reconciled with the community of the Church.

"Christ has willed that … his whole Church should be the sign and instrument of the forgiveness and reconciliation that he acquired for us at the price of his blood."[163]

Part of the plan laid out by God's providence is that we should fight strenuously against all sickness and carefully seek the blessings of good health. —Pastoral Care of the Sick, Rituale Romanum

During his earthly ministry, Christ appointed his disciples as ministers of the sacrament of penance and reconciliation when he said, "Receive the holy Spirit. Whose sins you forgive are forgiven them, and whose sins you retain are retained" (John 20:22–23). Today, "bishops who are their [the apostle's] successors, and priests, the bishops' collaborators, continue to exercise this ministry."[164] In fact:

> *When he celebrates the sacrament of Penance, the priest is fulfilling the ministry of the Good Shepherd who seeks the lost sheep, of the Good Samaritan who binds up wounds, of the Father who awaits the prodigal son and welcomes him on his*

---

163   *CCC* 1442.
164   *CCC* 1461.

> return, and of the just and impartial judge whose judgment is
> both just and merciful. The priest is the sign and the instrument
> of God's merciful love for the sinner.[165]

Through sin, suffering entered into the world, and Christ conquers
sin through the power of forgiveness. The *Catechism* tells us:

> "The whole power of the sacrament of Penance consists in restor-
> ing us to God's grace and joining us with him in an intimate
> friendship." Reconciliation with God is thus the purpose and
> effect of this sacrament. For those who receive the sacrament of
> Penance with contrite heart and religious disposition, reconcil-
> iation "is usually followed by peace and serenity of conscience
> with strong spiritual consolation." Indeed the sacrament of Rec-
> onciliation with God brings about a true "spiritual resurrection,"
> restoration of the dignity and blessings of the life of the children
> of God, of which the most precious is friendship with God.[166]

> **Anointing of the Sick:** One of the seven sacraments of the
> Church, consisting of an anointing with oil and the recitation
> of a specific formula, which is administered by a priest to a
> sick or dying person.

Just as the Church has a special rite for the forgiveness of sins, the
Church also has its own rite for the sick, as is witnessed by St. James:

---

165   CCC 1465.

166   CCC 1468, quoting *Roman Catechism*, II, V, 18; Council of Trent (1551): DS 1674. See
      Luke 15:32.

"Is anyone among you sick? He should summon the presbyters of the church, and they should pray over him and anoint [him] with oil in the name of the Lord" (James 5:14).

By this special rite, Christ makes his disciples share in his ministry. "So they went off and preached repentance. They drove out many demons, and they anointed with oil many who were sick and cured them" (Mark 6:12–13). However, the privilege of offering this sacrament is restricted. "Only priests (bishops and presbyters) are ministers of the Anointing of the Sick."[167] Also, "The recovery of health resulting from the Sacrament of Anointing of the Sick … is not a miraculous but a sacramental healing."[168]

Charism of Healing

While the Church appoints her priests to administer the sacraments of healing:

> The "charism of healing" is not attributable to a specific class of faithful. It is quite clear that St. Paul, when referring to various charisms in 1 Corinthians 12, does not attribute the gift of "charisms of healing" to a particular group, whether apostles, prophets, teachers, those who govern, or any other. The logic which governs the distribution of such gifts is quite different: "All these are activated by the one and the same

"The risen Lord renews this mission ('In my name…they will lay their hands on the sick, and they will recover.') and confirms it through the signs that the Church performs by invoking his name. These signs demonstrate in a special way that Jesus is truly 'God who saves.'" —CCC 1507

167   CCC 1516
168   Letter, pp. 960–961.

Spirit, who distributes to each one individually just as the Spirit chooses" (1 Corinthians 12:11)....[169]

This means that all lay persons are permitted and encouraged to offer general prayers for healing, and may operate in the charism of healing.

> **The Gift of Healing:** "The manifestation of the Spirit whereby a physical, psychological or spiritual healing or renewal occurs which is due primarily to God's action, although natural causes can be used."[170]

Healing is of three types:

> **Physical Healing:** "Whereby some disease of the body is remedied and the person, at least in this area, is returned to health. The number of healings which can occur corresponds to the list of possible diseases."[171]

> **Psychological Healing:** "Whereby some emotions or mental problems, usually associated with unhappy memories or unhealthy psychological attitudes, are alleviated. The healings in this area would correspond to the list of possible psychological problems."[172]

> **Spiritual Healing:** "Whereby some habit of sin or temptation is

---

169 Congregation for the Doctrine of the Faith, Instruction on Prayers for Healing, pt. I, no. 5.
170 Walsh, p. 75.
171 Walsh, p. 75.
172 Walsh, p. 75.

removed. The possible healings in this realm would correspond to the list of spiritual illnesses."[173]

A spiritual healing touches the normal spiritual problems that everyone faces—difficulty in Mass attendance, habit of sin, refusal to be reconciled to another, hostility, etc. Although somewhat akin to psychological healing, the person could very well be spiritually ill and emotionally very happy.

Practice has shown that frequently the psychological or even physical healing is withheld until the person yields to a spiritual healing being offered by God.[174]

"In sickness, God wants us to turn to Him and to those gifted with natural healing talents…. God's healing action supplements and completes the natural healing activity which man can carry out for himself." —Msgr. Vincent Walsh

Unlike the gift of personal prayer tongues, the charism of healing is a passing manifestation of the Holy Spirit.

> … The "ministry of healing" is not at all like the power of healing which a doctor possesses from a natural study and skill. The doctor's power is his own and he does attempt to cure all. A charismatic power is God's and the person is only an instrument….[175]

Natural and Supernatural Means

The charism of healing is most commonly associated with miraculous and instant cures, such as Jesus's cure of the man with leprosy (see Matthew 8:1–3) and the paralytic (Mark 2:2–12). However, the charism

---

173 Walsh, p. 75.
174 Walsh, p. 84.
175 *Key to the Catholic Charismatic Renewal*, Msgr. Vincent Walsh p 86

of healing is not limited to immediate and miraculous manifestations.

In the Book of Tobit, the archangel Raphael tells Tobias to rub fish gall on his father's eyes. When Tobias applies this medicine, his father, Tobit, is cured of blindness (see Tobit 11:4–14). The prophet Isaiah instructed King Hezekiah, who was near death, to prepare a "poultice of figs" and apply it on a boil, and he would live fifteen years longer (2 Kings 20:1–7). In each of these cases, the healing that occurred was indeed miraculous; however, it came through earthly remedies. Jesus illustrates this when he heals the man who was born blind by applying clay made from his spit and telling the man to wash in the pool of Siloam (John 9:6–7).

The Book of Sirach offers clear instructions on using natural means for healing as gifts from God:

> *God makes the earth yield healing herbs*
> *   which the prudent man should not neglect.*
> *Was not the water sweetened by a twig*
> *   so that all might learn his power?*
> *He endows people with knowledge,*
> *   to glory in his mighty works,*
> *Through which the doctor eases pain,*
> *   and the druggist prepares his medicines;*
> *Thus God's creative work continues without cease*
> *   in its efficacy on the surface of the earth.*
> *My son, when you are ill, do not delay,*
> *   but pray to God, for it is he who heals.*
> *Flee wickedness and purify your hands;*
> *   cleanse your heart of every sin.*
> *Offer your sweet-smelling oblation and memorial,*

> *a generous offering according to your means.*
> *Then give the doctor his place*
>   *lest he leave; you need him too.*
> *For there are times when recovery is in his hands.*
>   *He too prays to God*
> *That his diagnosis may be correct*
>   *and his treatment bring about a cure.*
> *Whoever is a sinner before his Maker*
>   *will be defiant toward the doctor. (Sirach 38:4–15)*

With this in mind, the healing charism can look very different in different situations. Just as healing can make a crippled man walk or a deaf man hear, it can also move an alcoholic to get help from an Alcoholics Anonymous group.

Safeguarding the Charism of Healing

The following notes help safeguard the charism of healing:

- The charism of healing is never to be treated as a personal possession, nor is it permissible to use the charism to draw attention to oneself.
- The manifestation of the charism is always at the disposal of the Lord for the building up of the Church.
- To avoid abuse and ensure the proper use of the charism, one must at all times remain obedient to Church authority.
- Test all words of knowledge concerning healing against sound doctrine and practical common sense before accepting them or sharing them.
- Pray with expectant faith, but leave the outcome in God's hands.

◆ Reflect. Receive. Respond.

- Have you ever witnessed or experienced a miraculous healing? What did God show you through that experience?
- In what areas of your life do you need physical, psychological, or spiritual healing?
- Ask God to reveal an individual for whom he desires you to pray for healing. How will you respond to his guidance? (See this session's practicum for specific directions.)

5.3

STEPS TO PRAYING FOR HEALING

Heal me, LORD, that I may be healed; save me, that I may be saved, for you are my praise. (Jeremiah 17:14)

The charism of healing typically manifests itself during intercessory prayer, which we discussed in session 2. As a reminder, intercessory prayer builds in three phases:

1. Preparation Phase
2. Prayer Phase
3. Post-Care Phase

Preparation Phase

Intercessory prayer begins long before one meets another and begins to pray for him or her. Our lives should be a continual preparation for intercessory prayer.

Session 2 offers some general guidelines for a prayer minister, such as being in a state of grace, having a regular prayer life, belonging to a prayer community, being free from addictions and compulsions, maintaining good personal hygiene, and having others interceding for you. Here are some added suggestions for healing prayer:

Purify your intentions: Strive to possess a spirit of humility and a servant's heart in your prayers for healing. Seek this mindset before you enter into prayer ministry. "All aspects of the human spirit should be removed—especially any desire to 'be in on the action' or 'to chalk up another one.'"[176]

Form a Team: The charism of healing typically draws on many other charismatic gifts, which when working together, have the effect of bringing about God's healing. "Since many gifts are used in healings," Msgr. Walsh tells us, "a team approach to this prayer is frequently recommended."[177]

For example, "The gift of the Word of Knowledge frequently can help the person understand what obstacles exist to being healed, or what God expects of him so that His action can occur."[178] And "the gift of discernment is needed to distinguish between the need for healing and the need for deliverance. Lack of discernment can frustrate God's action."[179]

---

176   Walsh, p. 85.
177   Walsh, p. 86.
178   Walsh, p. 86.
179   Walsh, p. 86.

Prayer Phase

Keep in mind the ten steps discussed in session 2 for praying with others. In prayers for healing, an additional step, "Offer Brief Instructions," is encouraged. Be prepared to adapt and make changes based on the culture, time restraints, and environment. (For a fuller description of each step, please refer to section 2.3 of session 2.)

THE 10 STEPS

1. The Initial Meeting
2. Ask Questions *Offer Brief Instructions*
3. Ask Permission
4. Invite the Presence & Offer Praise
5. Wait on the Spirit to Direct the Prayer
6. Pray in the Name of Jesus
7. Check for Results
8. Receive the Blessing of the Father
9. Seal the Prayer
10. Give Praise, Honor, and Glory to God

1. Initial Meeting

Establish contact, relationship, and the environment. Make introductions. If there are multiple people praying, appoint someone to act as leader of the prayer. Exude charity: "This charismatic gift [of healing] exists 'for others" and is manifested abundantly where love is obvious."[180]

---

180   Walsh, p. 85.

"[I]n modern days, He [Jesus] gives the power of the healing ministry to those who are compassionate and sensitive to others. Through their instrumentality, Jesus continues to show compassion toward mankind."[181]

> *The leader should make the initial introductions, such as, "Hi, it's nice to meet you. I'm glad you're here today. My name is _____, and this is _____ and _____; what is your name?" "Where are you from?" "Have you ever been prayed for by someone?"*

2. Ask Questions

Ask the individual what he or she would like the team to pray for. Briefly try to uncover the person's spiritual background. Is he or she familiar with the Holy Spirit and his manifestations? Be cautious if you suspect any associations with satanic or occult practices, as well as any addictions or compulsions. Ask about the person's pain level, on a scale of 1 to 10.

> *"What would you like us to pray for?" "Have you ever been part of a prayer team before?" "What's your spiritual background?" "Tell us about your injury; how did it happen?" "Have you received any prayer or treatment for this yet?"*

2.5 Offer Brief Instructions

In a spirit of charity and with a pastoral heart, the individual receiving prayers for healing "should be instructed before the prayer so his faith can be released."[182]

---

181 Walsh, p. 77.
182 Walsh, p. 85.

Faith is an extremely important element in the yielding to God's healing power....

On the part of the one praying for the healing, there must be a yielding to the charismatic gift of faith. On the part of the one prayed for, there is required only a normal faith (fruit of faith) which believes that God can and does heal.[183]

It is important to note, "Faith is not the *cause* of healing, but only a condition for a healing to take place. God alone is the cause of a healing."[184] The Congregation for the Doctrine of the Faith counsels, "[Not even the most intense prayer obtains the healing of all sicknesses."[185]

> *"Jesus has the power to overcome sickness and illness, and so I'm going to call upon his name and ask his Holy Spirit to heal you."*
> *"Will you pray with me that the Holy Spirit come upon you?"*
> *"Sometimes, even the most fervent prayers do not bring healing, but we are going to pray anyway."*

3. Ask Permission

Ask permission to pray for the person; to lay hands on him or her, perhaps at the site of an injury or ailment; or to use your prayer tongue. Direct contact, while helpful, is not necessary. Ask the person if you can pray for the Holy Spirit to come into his or her heart in a special way.

> *"Would you mind if I pray for you?" "Can I place my hand on your shoulder?" "Do you mind if I quietly pray in tongues?"*

---

183   Walsh, p. 85.

184   Walsh, p. 85.

185   Congregation for the Doctrine of the Faith, Instruction on Prayers for Healing, pt. I, no. 5.

4. Invite the Presence and Offer Praise

"Prayers of praise to God should precede, accompany and follow any prayer for healing."[186] Create an awareness of the presence of the Holy Spirit.

> *"Come, Holy Spirit, come" "Jesus, we thank you and praise you for the gift of XYZ."*

5. Wait on the Spirit to Direct the Prayer

Ask the Holy Spirit what you are to pray for. Ask the Holy Spirit to reveal any blocks to the desired healing. Wait on his direction.

> *"Lord, tell us how we are to pray" "Lord, reveal any blocks to healing that may be present."*

6. Pray in the Name of Jesus

Ask for healing in the name of Jesus. At this point, other gifts—such as prophecy, words of wisdom, discernment, and knowledge—may begin manifesting. Communicate with delicacy and charity, in a manner that honors the freedom and dignity of the person receiving prayer. If any deliverance prayer is in order, make sure the individual receiving prayer actually prays the deliverance prayer.

> *"In the name of Jesus, receive healing." "Lord, I ask that you bless XYZ with consolation in the name of Jesus." "In the name of Jesus,*

---

186   Walsh, p. 85.

I bind and renounce the spirit of anger." "In the name of Jesus,
grant XYZ the graces to desire to forgive."

7. Check for Results

Look to see if healing has occurred. Ask the individual if he or she
has received healing. If the answer is yes, test the healing with the
individual. Ask how much pain is still present, on a scale of 1 to 10.

If the person has not experienced healing, go back to step 5,
asking God if there are any blocks to healing.

> *"How are you doing?" "Can you tell me how you feel right now?"*
> *"Do you feel that God is doing anything within you right now?"*
> *"Would you like to continue praying?" "Are you comfortable*
> *trying to test for healing?"*

8. Receive the Blessing of the Father

Ask the individual to receive, "in the name of Jesus," the blessing of
the Father. Ask Jesus to fill any voids left from renounced lies and
sin, forgiveness, or banished sickness.

> *"In the name of Jesus, receive in abundance the Father's blessing."*
> *"Lord, enter into her heart and fill the voids with your blessing."*
> *"Jesus, where there was sin and regret, we ask that you fill those*
> *places of her heart and soul with your love and blessing."*

9. Seal the Prayer

Ask for God's mercy and anointing over the prayer session. Ask him to purify everything that was said or prayed. If any doors to evil have been closed, ask that God seal them shut and send angels to stand and protect these doors for all eternity. If the individual is Catholic, encourage him or her to seal the prayer in the sacrament of penance and reconciliation.

> *"Jesus, we ask that, for every door that was closed tonight, you send a guardian angel to guard it for all eternity." "We seal this prayer in Jesus's name."*

10. Give Praise, Honor, and Glory to God

Give praise to God. Thank him for any gift that manifested: words of knowledge, prophecy, discernment. Thank God for his consolations, healing, and all good gifts. Thank God for the opportunity to pray with this individual.

> *"Lord, we praise you, we thank you, and we glorify you for your mighty love for us." "Jesus, thank you for listening and responding to our prayer."*

Post-Care Phase

It is important to always consider the heart of the person you have been praying with. Sometimes our prayers are answered immediately; other times, the person may need follow-up care with other prayer ministries, a psychologist, or a counselor.

- If the individual claims to have received a healing, try to get contact information and an honest testimony. Contact the

person at a later date to verify that the healing is permanent
or to see if more prayer is in order. If the healing occurred at a
public place, the local bishop will want to be informed.

• Confidentiality must be maintained.

5.4

BLOCKS, CONSOLATIONS & CONFIRMATIONS

The crowds, meanwhile, learned of this and followed him. He received them and spoke to them about the kingdom of God, and he healed those who needed to be cured. (Luke 9:11)

Blocks to Healing

There are a few reasons why an individual may not receive healing immediately. It is good to keep in mind the following, as they may help to direct the prayer for healing.

> ***Unforgiveness.*** An individual may sometimes not be able to experience healing because of a lack of forgiveness. The Scriptures are clear: "If you forgive others their transgressions, your heavenly Father will forgive you. But if you do not forgive others, neither will your Father forgive your transgressions" (Matthew 6:14–15).

Need for Deliverance. The grace for healing can sometimes be blocked by demonic influences. These may be oppression, obsession, curses, or lies to be renounced. In these cases, prayer teams should review the five steps of deliverance prayer in section 3.5 of session 3.

Time. Some healings take place slowly (like a slow-release ibuprofen tablet). Some healings simply require a great deal of time, like the process of grieving the loss of a loved one. Particularly when deliverance is involved, healings might require "prayer and fasting" (Matthew 17:21).

Faith. While faith is not the *cause* of healing, it is a requirement for the healing to occur. "Faith or trust on the part of the sick is required as a condition for the cure; it is not its cause."[187] That being said, prayer teams should **never** blame a lack of healing on the lack of faith of the person being prayed for.

God's Will. There are cases in which "not even the most intense prayer obtains the healing."[188] This mystery is closely united to Christ's suffering on the cross.

In the end, where God is present, a healing always occurs. Even if unseen, unknown, or unrecognized, the presence of God always brings about some form of healing.

---

187   Letter, P.D. (1967). Christian Healing. *In the New Catholic Encyclopedia* (pp. 960-961). Washington, DC: McGraw-Hill.

188   Congregation for the Doctrine of the Faith, Instruction on Prayers for Healing, pt. I, no. 5.

Consolations

There are many signs and consolations that accompany a healing. Though not an exhaustive list, the following are common signs of the healing presence of the Holy Spirit.

> *The Gift of Tears.* One of the many consolations in healing ministry is the gift of tears. These tears, which are accompanied by the good fruits of the Holy Spirit, typically manifest when an individual has encountered the healing power of the Holy Spirit. This commonly occurs when:
>
> - a true word of knowledge, wisdom, or prophecy has been spoken;
> - the individual is moved by a profound sense of God's presence;
> - the individual experiences healing;
> - the person realizes "the burdens and anxieties that God wants to release."[189]
>
> *Warmth.* Many individuals report a sensation of warmth or electricity in the area that is receiving healing prayer. Similarly, those praying often report that their hands or bodies become unusually hot.
>
> *The Fruits of the Holy Spirit.* The individual and those praying report profound senses of peace, joy, and other fruits of the Holy Spirit.
>
> *Miraculous Healing.* The desired healing occurs. For example, a wound closes, a missing limb regrows, sight is restored.

---

189   Walsh, p. 83.

Confirmations

The following lists can help confirm that a healing has taken place:

Physical Healing
- The physical condition significantly or completely improves.
- The individual reports that he or she no longer feels pain or discomfort.

Psychological Healing
- The person experiences consolations, such as those listed in the previous section.
- "The person feels more content with himself."[190]
- "The physical symptoms accompanying the emotional disorder (as upset stomach, headaches, nervous tension) are also removed."[191]
- "The person feels more comfortable in personal relationships within family or at work."[192]

Spiritual Healing
- The person experiences consolations.
- The person has a renewed desire for prayer and the sacraments.
- The individual reports feeling closer or more intimate with God.

---

190   Walsh, p. 79.
191   Walsh, p. 79.
192   Walsh, p. 79.

5.5

GENERAL GUIDELINES FOR HEALING PRAYER

1. *"Be thankful and joyful*, but prudently cautious in verifying healings."[193]

2. At all times, *honor the free will* of the person you are praying for. Not everyone who needs help wants help.

3. *Focus on the immediate needs of the individual*, and pay attention to time constraints. Do not try to enter into in-depth counseling during a public prayer service.

4. *Encourage the individual to pray with you*, as opposed to passively listening and receiving your prayers. Avoid doing all the praying.

---

193   Doctrinal Commission of ICCRS, Guidelines on Prayers for Healing.

5.   Out of respect for the anointing of the sick, *the laity are not to anoint or bless anyone with oil.*

6.   *Put the Gospel message first.*

> *A very important connection exists between the two [healing and preaching the Gospel]. Healings, in the time of Jesus, were a confirmation of His preaching. He discouraged them as "goals" to be sought after, but tried to get the people to see them as "signs" of the kingdom and the importance of His message. The message was more important than the healing.*[194]

> *"Focus not so much on the healings as on the Divine Healer."*[195]

7.   *Understand the importance of faith.* If the individual you are praying for does not receive healing, do not shame him or her or say that the healing did not occur because of lack of faith.

> ... Sometimes people are told that God always wants to heal and that the reason people are sick is they do not have enough faith in God's action. This teaching has horrendous results and does not respect the divine mystery present in suffering.
>
> A person who believes this teaching begins to blame himself for remaining ill or ... strains to "work up" enough faith in order to *be* healed. These efforts are in vain, for

---

194 Walsh, p. 76.

195 Doctrinal Commission of ICCRS, Guidelines on Prayers for Healing.

healing is God's work among us and not our own.

Faith is not the *cause* of healing, but only a condition for a healing to take place. God alone is the cause of a healing.[196]

8. Regardless of the outcome, **do not be discouraged when you pray for God to heal.** "[N]ot even the most intense prayer obtains the healing of all sicknesses."[197]

9. *Lay persons are not permitted to give the anointing of the sick.*

Liturgical prayers for healing are celebrated according to the rite prescribed in the *Ordo benedictionis infirmorum* of the *Rituale Romanum* (28) and with the proper sacred vestments indicated therein.[198]

10. While St. Paul does say that only some receive the *ministry* of healing, **all Christians are encouraged to petition God for the healing of themselves and others.** "It is licit [permitted] for every member of the faithful to pray to God for healing."[199] James tells us to "pray for one another, that you may be healed. The fervent prayer of a righteous person is very powerful" (James 5:16).

11. As in the general guidelines for intercessory prayer, **the person**

---

196 Walsh, pp. 85–86.
197 Congregation for the Doctrine of the Faith, Instruction on Prayers for Healing, pt. I, no. 5.
198 Congregation for the Doctrine of the Faith, Instruction on Prayers for Healing, pt. II, art. 3 §1.
199 Congregation for the Doctrine of the Faith, Instruction on Prayers for Healing pt. II, art. 1.

of the highest office of authority is to be the leader of the group praying. This individual can choose to yield his or her authority to another person. When a healing service is "organized in a church or other sacred place, it is appropriate that such prayers be led by an ordained minister."[200]

For liturgical services to be valid, an ordained minister must lead. For non-liturgical healing services, it is most appropriate for a priest or deacon to preside, but this isn't mandatory.

Those who wish to put on a liturgical healing service must obtain the permission of the local bishop (or ordinary), even if the event includes the participation of other bishops or cardinals. Once permission is obtained, those hosting the event need to consult the diocese on liturgical norms. "The Diocesan Bishop has the right to issue norms for his particular Church regarding liturgical services of healing."[201]

12.   *Non-liturgical services are also under the vigilance of the local ordinary.* Participants must remain obedient to instructions, rules, and norms issued by the local ordinary for such events.

13.   *During prayer, avoid eccentricities.* "Anything resembling hysteria, artificiality, theatricality or sensationalism, above all on the part of those who are in charge of such gatherings, must not take place."[202]

14.   *Be aware, when seeking to film or televise a healing service,*

200   Congregation for the Doctrine of the Faith, Instruction on Prayers for Healing, pt. II, art. 1.

201   Congregation for the Doctrine of the Faith, Instruction on Prayers for Healing, pt. II, art. 4 § 1; see Canon 838 §4.

202   Congregation for the Doctrine of the Faith, Instruction on Prayers for Healing, pt. II, art. 5 § 3.

that "[t]he use of means of communication (in particular, television) in connection with prayers for healing, falls under the vigilance of the Diocesan Bishop."[203] This directive extends to all social media.

15. Concerning a person seeking healing: "***Do not assume responsibility for this person's life.*** A momentary plea for help is not an invitation to manage his or her life permanently."[204] You may intercede for the person in your personal prayer life, but remember that Jesus is the Savior, not you.

---

203 Congregation for the Doctrine of the Faith, Instruction on Prayers for Healing, pt. II, art. 6.

204 McNutt, F. (1998, March 16). Renouncing Occult Involvement. School of Healing Prayer. Jacksonville, Florida, United States.

practicum

FOR SESSION 5

THE 10 STEPS OF FACE-TO-FACE INTERCESSORY PRAYER

1. Meet
2. Ask Questions *Offer Brief Instructions*
3. Ask Permission
4. Invite the Presence & Offer Praise
5. Wait on the Spirit to Direct the Prayer
6. Pray in the Name of Jesus
7. Check for Results
8. Ask for the Blessing of the Father
9. Seal the Prayer
10. Give Praise, Honor, and Glory to God

THE 5 STEPS OF DELIVERANCE PRAYER

Repent

Forgive

Renounce

Take Authority

Ask for the Father's Blessing

exercise 1

PRAYERS FOR HEALING

Go rather to the lost sheep of the house of Israel. As you go, make this proclamation: "The kingdom of heaven is at hand." Cure the sick, raise the dead, cleanse lepers, drive out demons. Without cost you have received; without cost you are to give. (Matthew 10:6–8)

Directions:

Break into groups of three or four. Ask within your group if anyone needs healing. Have one volunteer agree to receive prayer. Use the Ten Steps of Face-to-Face Intercessory Prayer and, if called for, the Five Steps of Deliverance Prayer. Pray in teams. Remember to pray expectantly, with faith and perseverance.

After the prayer session, answer the following questions:

- Who is on your prayer team?
- Were any prophecies, words of knowledge, or words of wisdom revealed? Describe them.
- Were any non-prophecies shared?
- What consolations were present?
- Did the healing occur?
- What lesson did you learn about healing?

Notes:

_____

_____

_____

_____

_____

_____

_____

_____

_____

_____

_____

_____

Vocabulary

Addiction: An unhealthy attachment to a particular substance, object, or activity (for example, drugs, pornography, gambling, alcohol).

Anointing of the Sick: One of the seven sacraments of the Church, administered by a priest to a sick or dying person, to bring healing, comfort, and the forgiveness of sins.

Awakening of the Holy Spirit: See *Outpouring of the Holy Spirit.*

Baptism of the Holy Spirit: See *Outpouring of the Holy Spirit.*

Bind: To tie, fasten, or constrain. In deliverance ministry, asking Jesus to "bind a spirit" renders the evil spirit unable to manifest its power.

Charismatic Gift: A manifestation of God's power and presence given freely for God's honor and glory and for the service of others. Refers to manifestations of the power of the Holy Spirit mentioned in the Scriptures, especially after Pentecost, which have remained with the Church in both her teaching and practice.

Charisms: Graces of the Holy Spirit (whether extraordinary or simple and humble) that directly or indirectly benefit the Church, ordered as they are to her building up, to the good of men, and to the needs of the world.

Compulsion: Uncontrollable thoughts or impulses to perform an act.

Consolation: A sign from God that brings comfort, reassurance, support, or encouragement.

Curse: A solemn utterance intended to invoke a supernatural power to inflict harm or punishment on someone or something.

Deliverance: "A generic term for freeing someone from the influence of a demon, … applied specifically to cases of obsession, oppression of persons, and infestation of places."[205]

Deliverance Prayer: A form of intercessory prayer, the goal of which is to rescue or set a person free from demonic influence.

Demonization: The subjection of a person, place or thing to the influence of demons. This includes infestation, oppression, obsession, and possession.

Deprecative Formula: A prayer that petitions God to liberate a person from the influence of an evil spirit.

Directive Prophecy: A type of prophecy that tells a person to do something, such as intercede for someone, be aware of an upcoming problem, or avoid going somewhere.

Discernment (of Spirits), Gift of: "An illumination by God which enables the person to see through the outward appearance of an action

---

205 Leyshon, p. 5.

or inspiration in order to judge its source. Inspirations or actions can come from three sources (or 'spirits')—from God, from the person, or from the devil. Having correctly discerned the source, the person can then proceed in the situation with more wisdom"[206]

Effusion of the Holy Spirit: See *Outpouring of the Holy Spirit*.

Exorcism: "The act of driving out, or warding off, demons ... from persons, places, or things, which are believed to be possessed or infested."[207]

Faith, Gift of: A gift that enables a person to believe and to call upon God's power with a certainty that excludes all doubt.

Grave Sin: A serious offense against God "specified by the Ten Commandments, corresponding to the answer of Jesus to the rich young man: 'Do not kill, Do not commit adultery, Do not steal, Do not bear false witness, Do not defraud, Honor your father and your mother' [Mark 10:19]. The gravity of sins is more or less great: murder is graver than theft. One must also take into account who is wronged: violence against parents is in itself graver than violence against a stranger."[208]

Healing, Gift of: "The manifestation of the Spirit whereby a physical, psychological or spiritual healing or renewal occurs which is due primarily to God's action, although natural causes can be used."[209]

---

206 Walsh, p. 100.
207 Toner, Patrick. "Exorcism." The Catholic Encyclopedia. Vol. 5. New York: Robert Appleton Company, 1909. 11 Jun. 2017 <http://www.newadvent.org/cathen/05709a.htm>.
208 *CCC* 1858.
209 Walsh, p. 75.

Hex: A magic spell or curse.

Imperative Formula: A command addressed directly to an evil spirit—for example, "Be gone, Satan!"

Infestation (Demonic): "[T]he influence of evil spirits over objects, animals, houses, or places. These can become infested by exposure to occult activity or by a deliberate curse being directed towards them."[210]

Intercessory Prayer: A prayer petitioning God for intentions of another person. It knows no boundaries and extends to one's enemies.

Interpretation, Gift of: "The ... power given to an individual to speak, in the vernacular, the general meaning of whatever was said aloud in the gift of tongues."[211]

Laying on of Hands: See *Proximal Intercessory Prayer*.

Major Exorcism: The solemn rite of exorcism reserved for possessed persons.

Manifestation: The indication of the presence and nature of a spirit in a person or thing. Manifestations can be good (gift of tears and hot hands when praying for healing) or bad (yelling, seizing, and vomiting).

Minor Exorcism: A form of exorcism available to every Catholic,

---

210 Leyshon, p. 4.

211 Walsh, p. 53.

not just possessed persons. As with major exorcism, it is administered by an ordained person. However, a lay catechist, with approval
from the local ordinary, may perform a minor exorcism as part of
the Rite of Christian Initiation of Adults.

Montanist Heresy: A heresy popular in the second century, named
after its founder, Montanus. He taught that individuals giving prophetic utterances were possessed by the Holy Spirit and spoke not
as messengers of God but as persons possessed by God and unable
to resist. The heresy caused great division for many reasons, most
especially because of the incorrect teaching that a person's free will
could be denied through the exercise of the charism and because it
disregarded obedience to Church authority. For example, when a
prophecy conflicted with Church teaching, Montanists would take
the side of the prophecy, believing the false prophet to have authority higher than that of the Church.

Mortal Sin: A serious offense against God, which "results in the loss
of charity and the privation of sanctifying grace, that is, of the state
of grace. If it is not redeemed by repentance and God's forgiveness,
it causes exclusion from Christ's kingdom and the eternal death of
hell, for our freedom has the power to make choices for ever, with
no turning back."[212] It is a grave sin committed with full knowledge
and full consent of the sinner.

Obsession: "Demonic influence which seems to reside inside a
person, usually afflicting a certain area in a person's life in the
form of strong habitual temptations. A person may open oneself

---

212 CCC 1861.

to such influence by deliberately seeking the presence or power of evil spirits through witchcraft, Satanism, or fortune-telling (Ouija, tarot, etc.); demonic obsession may also occur through other grave sins which are not explicitly associated with the occult, e.g. sexual activity by consecrated or ordained persons pledged to celibacy. The obsessing spirit usually needs to be identified by name and cast out (i.e. commanded to leave) or bound (i.e. forbidden from exerting any further influence)."[213]

Occult: Activities involving or related to supernatural, mystical, or magical powers or phenomena whose origins and end are not the Trinitarian God.

Oppression (Demonic): "Demonic influence which seems to come from a person, causing heaviness, weariness, or discouragement. Oppressive spirits may be acquired through exposure to a heavy presence of evil: e.g. by participating in deliverance ministry, by coming into contact with items of witchcraft. Oppressive spirits may be dispelled by a simple command to leave in the name of Jesus."[214]

Outpouring of the Holy Spirit: "An internal religious experience (or prayer experience) whereby the individual experiences the risen Christ in a personal way. This experience results from a certain 'release' of the powers of the Holy Spirit, usually already present within the individual by Baptism and Confirmation"[215] Also called awakening of the Holy Spirit, effusion of the Holy Spirit, and baptism of the Holy Spirit.

---

213 Leyshon, p. 4.

214 Leyshon, p. 4.

215 Walsh, p. 24.

Penance and Reconciliation: One of the seven sacraments of the Church, whereby a member of the faithful confesses sins to a priest, obtains divine mercy for those sins, and is reconciled with the Church.

Pentecostalism: A movement within Protestant Christianity that places a special emphasis on a direct, personal experience with God through the outpouring of the Holy Spirit.

Personal Prayer Tongue: One of two manifestations of the charismatic gift of tongues. (See *Tongues, Gift of*.) This permanent gift can be used at will by the individual and is considered a doorway to receiving other gifts of the Holy Spirit. In contrast to the gift of public tongues, a personal prayer tongue is meant for the individual, not for the public assembly.

Personal Prophecy: A prophecy, given either publicly or privately, meant exclusively for an individual rather than an entire group.

Physical Healing: The remedy of a disease of or injury to the body.

Possession (Demonic): The rarest of demonic attacks, which "occurs when human beings willfully hand over complete control of their life to Satan, by expressly doing so or by embracing grave sin. Formal exorcism, sanctioned by the diocesan bishop, is always required in such cases…. [Possession] is characterized by spectacular features in which the demon takes control, in a certain manner, of the strength and physical abilities of the person possessed. It cannot, however, take over the free will of the subject, so the demon cannot force the person possessed to choose to sin."[216]

---

216 Leyshon, p. 4.

Prayer: The raising of one's mind and heart to God or the requesting of good things from God.

Prayer Tongues: See *Tongues, Gift of.*

Private Prophecy: A form of prophecy that is shared with a single individual or a closed group, such as a small prayer group.

Prophecy, Gift of: "[A] gift whereby God manifests to man His own thoughts so that a message may be given for the individual or for a group of individuals, or for the community."[217]

Proximal Intercessory Prayer (PIP): Direct-contact prayer on behalf of someone, frequently involving touch, by one or more persons; more commonly known as "laying on of hands."

Psychological Healing: Alleviation of emotional or mental problems, "usually associated with unhappy memories or unhealthy psychological attitudes."[218]

Public Prayer Tongues: A "passing manifestation of the Holy Spirit to an individual … during a charismatic prayer meeting, whereby the person is prompted to speak aloud in tongues, which must be followed by use of the companion gift of interpretation. This use of the gifts of tongues and interpretation is very akin to the gift of prophecy."[219] See *Tongues, Gift of.*

---

217 Walsh, p. 60.

218 Walsh, p. 75.

219 Walsh, p. 51.

Public Prophecy: Prophecy that is shared in a public forum, such as a prayer service that has been advertised to the public.

Rebuke: To express sharp disapproval or criticism.

Reconciliation, Sacrament of: See *Penance and Reconciliation*.

Renounce: Formally declare one's abandonment of something or someone.

Resting in the Spirit: A form of religious ecstasy in which an individual falls to the floor.

Slain in the Spirit: A less preferable term for "resting in the Spirit."

Spiritual Healing: An action of God "whereby some habit of sin or temptation is removed. The possible healings in this realm ... correspond to the list of spiritual illnesses."[220] "A spiritual healing touches the normal spiritual problems that everyone faces—difficulty in Mass attendance, habit of sin, refusal to be reconciled to another, hostility, etc. Although somewhat akin to psychological healing, the person could very well be spiritually ill and emotionally very happy. Practice has shown that frequently the psychological or even physical healing is withheld until the person yields to a spiritual healing being offered by God."[221]

---

220   Walsh, p. 75.
221   Walsh, p. 85.

Tears, Gift of: Tears accompanied by the good fruits of the Holy Spirit, typically manifest when an individual has encountered the healing power of the Holy Spirit.

Tongues, Gift of: "[A] gift whereby the person prays to God in a language which he does not know, by simply 'yielding' to the action of the Holy Spirit.

"When 'praying in tongues,' the person does not use his rational powers of memory or intellect which are usually employed in speaking or praying. He does use the other faculties associated with speech—the lips, the tongue and the larynx."[222]

See *Personal Prayer Tongue* and *Public Prayer Tongues*.

Venial Sin: Sin that does not destroy God's life in the soul but diminishes it.

One commits *venial sin* when, in a less serious matter, he does not observe the standard prescribed by the moral law, or when he disobeys the moral law in a grave matter, but without full knowledge or without complete consent.[223]

Word of Knowledge: An insight into a divine mystery or facet of man's relationship to God, expressed in a way that helps others grasp the mystery.

Word of Wisdom: An insight into God's plan in a given situation, put into words of advice or of direction.

---

222 Walsh, p. 33.
223 *CCC* 1862.

Made in the USA
Columbia, SC
11 June 2022